ABOLITION *&* THE UNDERGROUND RAILROAD

in

VERMONT

Michelle Arnosky Sherburne

THE
History
PRESS

Published by The History Press
Charleston, SC 29403
www.historypress.net

Front cover: Webster sisters. *Courtesy of Bard and Gina Prentiss, tintype in private collection.*
Back cover: Slave collar. *Courtesy of Eric Francis, collar in Steve Leninski private collection.*
Titus Hutchinson House, Woodstock, Vermont. *Photo by Michelle Arnosky Sherburne.*
Norwich map. *Courtesy of Dave Allen and www.old-maps.com.*

First published 2013
Second printing 2014

Manufactured in the United States

ISBN 978.1.62619.038.2

Library of Congress Cataloging-in-Publication Data

Sherburne, Michelle Arnosky.
Abolition and Vermont's underground railroad / Michelle Arnosky Sherburne.
pages cm
Includes bibliographical references and index.
ISBN 978-1-62619-038-2
1. Antislavery movements--Vermont--History--19th century. 2. Underground Railroad--
Vermont--History--19th century. 3. Abolitionists--Vermont--History--19th century. I. Title.
E445.V4S54 2013
306.3'6209743--dc23
2013029162

This book is dedicated in memory of my grandmother Mary Eshleman, | who loved to read anything I wrote.

CONTENTS

ACKNOWLEDGEMENTS

This has been a twenty-one-year journey of delving into the history of Vermont's Underground Railroad for me, and it has kept me captivated.

First and foremost, I thank my husband, Rodney, and son Darren for all their love, support, encouragement and longstanding patience through years of research. To my father and mother, Jim and Deanna Arnosky, thank you for a lifetime of encouragement, love and guidance and for being my constellations.

I have many others to thank: Jutta Scott and Peacham Historical Association for the opportunity to work on their Civil War book project; Peter and Jackie Sinclair for their enthusiasm for my subject and facilitating opportunities for me to lecture; to Ellie Dixon and the *Caledonian-Record* for that first newspaper assignment about a Haverhill, New Hampshire Underground Railroad safe house that started a lifelong quest; and Connie Sanville, my employer and friend who has given me flexibility to pursue this endeavor.

And thanks go to the wonderful assistance of Bard and Gina Prentiss; Don Papson; Kathy Valloch; Chris Burns at University of Vermont Special Collections; Marjorie Strong and Vermont Historical Society; Steve Leninski; Eric Francis; Donna Zani-Dunkerton of Canaan Historical Society; Martha Howard of Thetford Historical Society; Jennifer Donaldson of Woodstock Historical Society; Jane Williamson of Rokeby Museum; David Warden of Barnet Historical Society; Betty Johnson Gray; Laura Osborn of *Upper Valley Life*; Robert Pelletier; John Burbank; Susan Ferland of Vergennes Historical

Society; Ed Pospicil and Joie Winchell; my sister Amber Maccini for her support; John Fatherley for his history kinship; Denise Williams White and Rosemarie Gillespie; my church family for their support; and Lorna Renfrew for our New York trip and searching for Noah's gravestone in the dark.

Charles E. Metz, architect, is responsible for the beautiful illustrations in this book, and I thank him for his time and patience. Also thanks to Dave Allen of www.old-maps.com whose work with making the Beers, Wallings and Hosea Doton maps available made researching easier. Lastly, thank you to my editor, Whitney Landis, who has helped me stay on track during this project.

It has been a privilege to learn about incredible people who made sacrifices for the Underground Railroad cause. It has been exciting to share about history and make it come to life for others.

Introduction

APPROACH TO UNDERGROUND RAILROAD RESEARCH

We are in the midst of the 150th celebrations of the Civil War, and the Underground Railroad played an important part in our country's prewar politics and tension. New Civil War artifacts, documents and memorabilia keep surfacing just as new information about the Underground Railroad does. These discoveries give us a better understanding of our country's history.

The Underground Railroad is an intriguing subject that captures the attention and imagination of young and old. It has all the components of an adventure thriller with the ultimate great ending—freedom for the slaves.

But researching is difficult because of the secrecy and lack of documentation. Researchers do not find complete details like ledger books of fugitives aided or operation details. The Underground Railroad was not about meetings, maps, manuals and membership. The Underground Railroad was a network of people who worked for a common cause within their area. People helped fugitive slaves from one place to another. Once a plan was established, it was used repeatedly, and thus it became organized. That's the extent of the organization of the Underground Railroad.

People helped strangers because they knew it was the right thing to do. Today, people who help others selflessly receive their "fifteen minutes of fame" with an interview on CNN or multiple hits on YouTube or Facebook. The heroes who helped the fugitives on their journey didn't get any recognition. All they received was the satisfaction that they had helped. They did their part, and it was out of their hands after that.

Researching the subject is like putting together a large puzzle of safe houses, towns, operators, routes, safety areas and contact information in which the pieces are scattered throughout the Northern states. It is the historian's task to gather and reconstruct the history.

We work with the pieces we discover—a single journal entry, a story from an agent's son, local tradition referring to runaways passing through town, a house with a secret tunnel entrance, an agent's letter to a fellow agent about a fugitive on the way. We investigate the clues and leads to determine if there is a connection to the Underground Railroad network. Granted, not every hidden closet or house by a train track was part of the Underground Railroad.

As new accounts and information surface, they shed more light on a realistic picture of nineteenth-century Vermont in terms of the abolitionist movement and the Underground Railroad. Vermont was known as the safe, friendly state, but it was full of intolerance for abolitionists, mobocracy and prejudice against blacks.

We will take a temperature reading of nineteenth-century America and apply it to researching history. We have to remember the time period these people lived in. We can't take the way we think in the twenty-first century and use it to understand history.

Difficulties arise when dealing with the Underground Railroad in New England and especially Vermont because misconceptions exist about Underground Railroad activity. The consensus is that New England was so far north that fugitives were safe and danger nonexistent because they were beyond the reach of their masters and slave catchers.

Through the years, skeptics have tried to change the image of the Underground Railroad. Larry Gara wrote *The Liberty Line*, which downplayed the role that white abolitionists played in the Underground Railroad and promoted the theory that Underground Railroad memories are no more than exaggerated stories from elderly citizens. Some historians take information out of context and surmise that a new perspective and focus must be applied to the subject based on fragments of information. The problem is that their studies are devoid of context; they ignore the contemporary conditions in the rest of the country, and this is problematic.

The fact is that New England states were no different than any other free states in the Union. The free states that had abolished slavery were Iowa, Illinois, Wisconsin, Indiana, Ohio, Pennsylvania, New Jersey, New York, Vermont, Connecticut, Rhode Island, Massachusetts, New Hampshire and Maine. Freed blacks and escaped slaves lived in each of these states.

Despite the skepticism about Vermont's role in the Underground Railroad, the information that exists shows that fugitive slaves traveled through the state on a regular basis. Someone had to be there to help them. We know that the Rowland Robinson farm was a documented Underground Railroad safe house.

When I began my research twenty years ago, I read every book about the Underground Railroad nationally, and Vermont kept cropping up. I kept running into references about Vermont towns or fugitives traveling from New Hampshire into Vermont or New York into Vermont. The basic elements of news reporting kicked into gear.

When a town was mentioned, I had to find out the who, what, when, where and how. I learned that cross-referencing was key in learning how people were connected. I would find a phrase like "a teacher from Vermont, Delia Webster" or "Springfield, Vermont" referenced in a book about the Underground Railroad. It took piecing together information to learn more about that reference.

The forerunner in researching the Underground Railroad was Wilbur Siebert. Born in 1866, he was a University of Ohio professor who collected and recorded a history of the Underground Railroad throughout the country. He wrote numerous books, including *The Underground Railroad from Slavery to Freedom* and *Vermont's Anti-Slavery and Underground Railroad Record*.

Siebert interviewed and corresponded with thousands of people across the country. He was fortunate to get information from people who had been involved personally or were eyewitnesses to fugitive slaves and also from families of Underground Railroad operators. He recorded testimonies of thousands of eyewitness accounts and gathered stories that had been passed down a generation. It is through Siebert's work that the concepts of how the Underground Railroad agents operated came together.

Another key source of information was William Still, a free black man who was instrumental in the Philadelphia Vigilance Committee, which aided thousands of fugitive slaves. He kept records of the people he met and their stories and published *The Underground Railroad* in 1878. Autobiographies by Frederick Douglass, Calvin Fairbank and Levi Coffin and work by R.C. Smedley and so many other works provide us with invaluable information about this network.

Unfortunately, not every fact is divulged because of the clandestine nature of the subject. We use the facts we do have to create a facsimile of what we think was the manner in which escaped slaves were aided. Understanding the culture and laws of the time help us relate to the risk and danger that Underground Railroad agents encountered.

Laws supported slave owners and the right to their property—the slaves. As early as 1787, the United States Constitution held that a slave was property, and when one ran away from his owner, the owner had a legal right to retrieve his property. It was illegal for any person to help a fugitive slave, and if caught in the act, they could be convicted to jail time or pay hefty fines.

The North wanted slavery to end but not if it would divide the country. There were abolitionists who believed that the only way to solve the slavery issue was to end it completely. The question at the time was how to do that.

There were varying shades of abolition as the 1800s progressed, from the passive to the immediate elimination at any cost. Today we use the terms "abolitionist" and "antislavery" interchangeably. Anyone against slavery must be an abolitionist because anyone who thought slavery was wrong would want to get rid of it. That was not the case in the 1800s.

The concepts of how to free the slaves were where the differences existed. Should it be by changing laws only, by force and violence against slave owners, by immediate emancipation, by colonization and shipping them out of the country or by a gradual emancipation so that it was slow influx of blacks coming North rather than a sudden rush.

Abolition meant eliminating the slavery institution and freeing all slaves. Most abolitionists wanted equality for blacks. They were against the Constitution, which allowed slavery. Standing up against the government and its laws made them traitors, troublemakers and radicals.

The Reverend Nathan R. Johnston worked for the abolitionist cause as a lecturer, preacher and Underground Railroad agent in Vermont, Indiana and Ohio. He wrote in *Looking Back from the Sunset Land*, "They call me 'traitor' because I have testified against the infidelity and pro-slavery character of this government."

Antislavery meant being against the concept of slavery. Some did not approve of slavery but didn't want to shake up the Union by upsetting the Southern faction. It was possible for one to be antislavery but not think blacks were equal.

The Reverend Joshua Young angered his Burlington, Vermont parishioners in 1854 with his sermon against slavery after he witnessed the runaway slave Anthony Burns's capture in Boston, Massachusetts. Young stated that Northerners were to blame for the perpetuation of slavery because of their willingness to return runaways to their Southern masters.

Young wrote that those who dared to speak against it were "branded as fanatics, thrown out of office, dismissed from their parishes, politically proscribed, socially ostracized," and Young knew that firsthand.

Though the lines were blurred in the antislavery faction back then, today we know these facts: approximately five hundred thousand people were captured from Africa and brought to the United States during the slave trade. In the early 1800s, attitudes worldwide about slavery were negative. Canada, England and Spanish-territory Florida had abolished slavery.

Vermont was the first state to abolish slavery in 1777. In 1808, the U.S. Congress banned the import of Africans to the States. In 1827, New York State passed the final Gradual Emancipation Act that freed the last of the slaves within the state. By 1837, slavery was abolished in all Northern states. By the beginning of the Civil War in 1861, there was a slave population of four million in the country. In 1863, President Abraham Lincoln issued the Emancipation Proclamation, freeing slaves in the Confederate states. In 1865, slavery was abolished with the Thirteenth Amendment.

No matter what the details of the Underground Railroad, we need to remember that forty thousand fugitive slaves escaped slavery, either landing in Canada or Northern states or leaving the country. The slaves were fearless in their desire for freedom. The slaves were the true heroes. And there were people willing to help them along the way, which was heroic as well. That's the bottom line. Whether it was in secret or riding in an open wagon during the day, the slaves were en route to a better life, and someone helped them. Vermonters need to be recognized for the part they played in this self-sacrificing cause.

Part I

VERMONT, ABOLITION
AND ANTISLAVERY

Chapter 1

NINETEENTH-CENTURY AMERICA

In the 1800s, the United States faced major growing pains politically and socially. Along with slavery, the issues of temperance, anti-Mason scares and spiritualism added to the brewing pot. The country was growing rapidly, and people were migrating west to new territories. Technology, transportation, science and industry were evolving. New states were forming and were volleyed between the free and slave states.

The dividing factor between the North and South was the slavery issue. The more the North tried to limit the expansion of slavery in new territories and states, the more Southerners became indignant, leaning toward separating themselves in the Secessionist movement.

Politically, if new territories were added as slave states to the Union, then the scales wouldn't be equal. It is similar to the balance of power today in Washington between the Democrats and Republicans. So with new states, the North wanted to have the advantage and add them to its team.

In free states, tension existed within the Northern attitudes on slavery, prejudice and racism and created challenges for abolitionists and Underground Railroad agents. Everything was percolating, and it was only a matter of time before it exploded. Would the "United" States stay that way or become two separate countries? All that tension was evident in everyday life, politics and in the media. Examining these factors allows us to understand what it was like for them.

NORTHERN ATTITUDES ABOUT SLAVERY

The majority of Northerners were against the concept of slavery, but they didn't think it was really their business. It didn't affect them personally, so slavery wasn't their problem. They were more interested in keeping the status quo in the country to save the Union. They would shake their heads at slavery, but they remained lukewarm, refusing to take a stand against the South.

The free states were involved with the slave states in trade and commerce, so they didn't want to affect their source of supplies. Abolishing slavery would force the South to give up their economy, culture and way of life. All New England states had commercial ties to the South, no matter how far north.

Many Northerners were of the mindset that they didn't want blacks flooding their towns. Most Northerners were antislavery but, at the same time, racist. Vermonters were the same.

NEW ENGLAND COMMUNITIES AND CHURCH INFLUENCE

The landscape of the towns in 1800s Vermont was very different from what it is today. In the 1800s, each community was self-sufficient because travel took too long and was difficult. Towns had to have businesses that provided jobs and supplies like feed stores, doctors, general stores, hotels and lumber mills. Residents did not travel twenty to thirty miles to get supplies. Employment was in town, not like today, with many having to travel fifty miles to commute to work.

People lived, worked, worshiped, shopped, banked, did business and socialized in one area with the same people. Because their world was very small, everything was connected.

The center of every community was the church, and its authority and influence was powerful. Even if you had more than one church in town, the role was the same. People were influenced and regulated by the church. In the 1800s, letters of introduction from a pastor were necessary to be accepted into a new community.

In the nineteenth century, church denominations were growing across the new nation. Presbyterian, Methodist, Lutheran and Quaker churches were sending ministers all over the country to start churches, which were popping up all over the country, keeping up with the fast-growing population of Americans.

In nineteenth-century America, speaking out about abolition made you a radical and unpatriotic. If you pushed your antislavery beliefs on people, they would shun you, and that meant your business and social life would be affected. Today, we don't understand what it means to be shunned, ostracized or excommunicated from Protestant churches (though the Catholic church still excommunicates members). One's wife, children, parents and the rest of the family would be affected as well.

Peacham Congregational Church and Leonard Johnson provide a perfect example of the church's discipline. Peacham had one of the first antislavery societies, established in 1833, and was known as an antislavery town. But the community did not tolerate outspoken abolitionists.

Johnson was a farmer who was open about his abolitionist views. In Charles A. Clark's *The Vermonter* article of September 1938, titled "Capt. Leonard's Confession," he wrote, "On one of these days the arguments grew fiercer than usual: so fierce, in fact, did the heat of the debate wax, that Johnson made remarks which his neighbor called an insult and unworthy of a church member. The matter was brought before the church and much discussion held. A strong effort was made to get Johnson to apologize to his neighbor for the remarks. Since Johnson would not acknowledge any wrong on his part, the church took his name off the rolls."

He was kicked out of the church for arguing about the antislavery issue. It wasn't until years later that his family learned that he had hid

Known for his outspoken abolitionist beliefs, Leonard Johnson of Peacham, Vermont, is buried in the Peacham Cemetery. His gravestone refers to him as "Capt. Leonard Johnson," and he died at ninety-three years old in 1890. Johnson was an Underground Railroad agent who lived north of Peacham Village. He was excommunicated from the Peacham Congregational Church for arguing with a fellow member about the slavery issue. *Courtesy of Michelle Arnosky Sherburne, 2013.*

fugitive slaves en route to Canada. The church and community also did not know that he was harboring fugitives.

On the day of John Brown's 1859 execution for his militant raid at Harper's Ferry, Virginia, abolitionist supporters across the North showed their support for Brown by tolling church bells, which was considered an act of defiance. Following suit, when news of Brown's execution reached Peacham, Johnson tolled the church bells for an hour. His bell tolling upset the community even more.

Johnson was finally persuaded to apologize two years after the Civil War. He conceded to sign a confession dated November 1, 1867, that was written by the minister and had Johnson's signature on it.

> *To the Congregational Church of Christ in Peacham*
> *Dear Brethren,*
>
> *The exclusion of myself from the fellowship of this church has been a source of much grief to myself and family. I love the church of Christ and desire to be identified with its members in promoting all its interests. I have had some hurt feelings because I thought I was treated unkindly by some of the brethren. I have said some things which I know were not very pleasant. I thought at the time that I was justified in so doing...I at least am ready to forgive what I think has been wrong & I ask to be forgiven for whatever others may have esteemed to be wrong in me. The principles which led me to do as I have done. I still think were right—viz. The principles of antislavery so called. My words may sometimes have been sharper than our self-denying & meek Master would have dictate.-*

The postscript in Johnson's handwriting states: "Yet I know the anti Slavery cause owed me but verry [*sic*] little, yet, I feel that I am greatly indebted to the cause, for, I feel it has been good for me to labor for the poor and down troden [*sic*] in our land." He still had the last word, with his postscript basically saying, "I'm not sorry for what I did for the cause."

As far north as Vermont, the antislavery movement faced strong opposition, even from religious institutions.

VERMONT, A PARADOX

Historically, Vermont was known as the "antislavery state" and that impression makes it seem like every citizen in the Green Mountain state opened their homes to fugitive slaves, blacks and abolitionists. But this was not true, and in reality, Vermont contradicted itself on all fronts.

Vermont was confusing because politically it was an antislavery state, the first state to abolish slavery. By 1837, there were eighty-nine antislavery societies in Vermont towns with over ten thousand members. Vermont had eleven antislavery newspapers from the 1830s to 1860s. Nationally known abolitionists William Lloyd Garrison, Oliver Johnson and Horace Greeley all got their newspaper training in Vermont.

The Vermont Antislavery Society was formed in 1834 with one hundred delegates from thirty different towns. Among the leadership was Underground Railroad agent Rowland T. Robinson of Ferrisburgh serving as chairman; clerk, Oliver Johnson; and Underground Railroad agent Asa Aldis of St. Albans, president. Other Underground Railroad operators in the membership were Lawrence Brainerd of St. Albans, Colonel Jonathan Peck Miller of Montpelier, Rodney Marsh of Brandon and Joseph Poland of Montpelier.

Garrison helped the abolitionist movement grow with his campaign against slavery, his *Liberator* antislavery newspaper and his lectures. He traveled around promoting the elimination of slavery through immediate emancipation. He helped establish numerous antislavery societies in the North.

At the antislavery conventions, fugitive slaves shared their stories. It was the free blacks and fugitive slaves like Henry Highland Garnet, Parker Pillsbury, Frederick Douglass, William Wells Brown and Solomon Northrup who shared firsthand experiences, while white abolitionists like Garrison, Benjamin Lundy, the Reverend George Storrs and Oliver Johnson pushed for immediate emancipation.

Vermont didn't always welcome and support abolitionist lecturers. Fugitive slave, Underground Railroad agent and abolitionist lecturer Frederick Douglass wrote in *Life and Times of Frederick Douglass Written by Himself* 1893: "Upon the whole, however, the several towns visited showed that Vermont was surprisingly under the influence of the slave power. Her proud boast that within her borders no slave had ever been delivered up to his master, did not hinder her hatred to anti-slavery."

Douglass thought Vermont was under the influence of the slave power? Vermont was a paradox because, despite its antislavery laws, actual Vermonters were not supportive of abolitionists and blacks.

Another example of a Vermont contradiction was an 1829 petition circulated by Garrison to abolish slavery with 2,352 Vermont signatures. Garrison presented the petition in Congress. Twenty years later, the temperature reading in Vermont had changed drastically, and Garrison expressed discouragement because of the Vermont freeze-out he experienced.

If Vermont was a free and safe place for fugitive slaves and blacks, then why wasn't there a large population of blacks during the span of 1830 to 1850? Nationally, in 1860, there were twenty-seven million whites and four million slaves.

According to the 1860 Census records, there were 315,000 whites in Vermont and 709 blacks. In Burlington, the numbers over a thirty-year period didn't change much regarding black population. In 1830, there were 3,500 whites and 53 blacks. By 1860, there were 7,700 whites in Burlington and 46 blacks.

Conversely, there were 40,000 black "refugees" in Canada by 1860. They had fled to the country where slavery was illegal.

Chapter 2

ABOLITIONISTS UNWELCOME IN VERMONT

When one reads the 1800s Vermont town histories or newspapers, the agitation and violence is vividly described. Across the entire country, the volume of violence during the antebellum era was alarming. It has been assumed that these tensions did not happen in Vermont and farther north.

Abolitionist lecturers traveled the Northern states rallying support for their movement. In New England, the circuit encompassed Massachusetts, Maine, New Hampshire, New York, Connecticut, Rhode Island and Vermont. In the early 1830s and 1840s in Vermont, antislavery conventions were held in Middlebury, Ferrisburgh, Waterbury, Bradford, West Randolph and Montpelier.

In some Vermont towns, abolitionists were welcomed. But in other towns, the atmosphere they faced was the opposite. Threats, violence and riots broke out around Vermont just like in Pennsylvania, New York or Massachusetts when abolitionists lectured. People didn't want to hear it. There was enough resentment against them because they were viewed as stirring up trouble. Many times, opponents would resort to violence to stop lectures.

Abolitionist lecturers or ministers who preached against slavery were physically threatened, which was serious business, not to be taken lightly. The famous Connecticut abolitionist Reverend Samuel May wrote a letter in 1857 to Topsham, Vermont abolitionist minister Reverend Nathan R. Johnston, conveying his goal of traveling around Vermont to spread abolitionism:

We wish to have the people of Vermont understand, better than they do now, the real character of our movement, the reasons of our "No Union" position, both

The Reverend Nathan R. Johnston was an Ohio native who served as pastor of the Topsham Presbyterian Church in Topsham, Vermont, from 1852 to 1864. He was friends with major players in the Abolitionist cause like William Lloyd Garrison, William Still, Levi Coffin, Oliver Johnson and the Reverend Samuel May. Johnston aided fugitive slaves while living in Indiana prior to moving to Vermont. He also traveled to Port Royal, South Carolina, to preach to contraband slaves during the Civil War. *Courtesy of* Looking Back From the Sunset Land or People Worth Knowing, *by Reverend N.R. Johnston, 1898.*

in the matters of state and church, and why it is that we have got ourselves so proscribed and odious, why it is that we are accounted infidel....No movement (in my humble judgment) ever had a clearer foundation in reason, common sense, the fundamental principles of morals, and the whole genius of Christianity, than our movement. As such, we wish to have the people understand it, and cease to be duped and misled by the tricksters who now sit in editorial chairs, mount political stumps and preach in professedly Christian pulpits.

"Duped and misled by tricksters" in the media, in the legislature and in church pulpits! Those are strong words about the country's authoritative powers. But May was concerned that the public was being brainwashed.

In the nineteenth century, most churches in the North did not take a stand against the institution of slavery. We think of church as sanctuary for those in trouble or in need of help. But at that time, church was not the place to share your abolitionist views. Some ministers played a role in helping runaway slaves, but it was secret work, not a church-supported activity.

The American church conferences connected the North and South, and the church's power and influence was prevalent. The churches did agree that slavery was bad, but that was the extent of their action on the subject. Half the members of their congregations were in the South, and they would be calling them evil and sinners. That would alienate half of their church membership. So the churches refused to support the abolitionist movement.

In March 20, 1840 issue of *The Liberator*, there was an article about the Vermont Antislavery Society and Clergy that stated: "The following resolution was adopted by the Vermont Antislavery Society: 'That those ministers who, with all the light they now enjoy in regard to the sinfullness (*sic*) of the slaveholder and the suffering of the slave, oppose the cause of emancipation, or remain silent on the subject, are unworthy of support or of confidence as religious guides and teachers.'"

So instead of abolitionists finding an ally in the church, they found churches refusing to stand against slavery.

An example of the church's intolerance for abolitionists occurred in Littleton, New Hampshire, which is over the eastern border of Vermont. Littleton abolitionists Nathan Allen and Erastus Brown attempted to address the antislavery issue during church services. But the congregation considered them troublemakers and unpatriotic. On a number of occasions, they tried to discuss it, but the minister refused. Finally, the minister had Allen and Brown dragged out of the building during the church service. They were arrested, put on trial and imprisoned. After they served their sentences, Allen and Brown left town. They wanted to educate people about slavery and get them to understand the abolitionist movement, but the church would not allow it.

Concerning the church's tolerance of slavery, *The History of Littleton, NH* states: "The clergy everywhere, with very few exceptions, closed every door, over which they had control, against all radical, effective Anti-Slavery truth. Some could rebuke slavery in words; but to break sacramental fellowship with slaveholders and their Northern accomplices, was not in all their thought. A thousand times they denounce slavery as 'the sum of all villainies.' But to declare persistent slave-breeders and slaveholders the sum of all villains, they dared not, or did not do."

VERMONT MOBOCRACY: "SILENCE THE ABOLITIONISTS!"

If tomorrow's newspaper arrived and you read headlines like "Death Threats after Abolitionist's Lecture in Topsham" or "Speaker Hosed During Antislavery Talk in Bradford," what would your impression be? Would you want to visit that state? If you were a fugitive slave and heard these stories, would you think it was a safe place to settle?

These events really happened. Not in Boston, Massachusetts, or Albany, New York, but in Vermont.

After the West Randolph, Vermont antislavery convention, Garrison wrote his wife on August 26, 1858, that the abolitionist lecturers were having difficulty finding a venue for the event. He wrote, "We could not obtain any meeting-house in the place so 'anti-Garrisonian' are the churches here, and so we had to go into a hall connected with the tavern, used for dancing and other purposes." A dance hall for an antislavery convention? That was like having a church conference in a bar.

ABOLITIONISTS FACED OPPOSITION even if they were just traveling from one town to another. In October 1862, Oliver Johnson and Garrison were on a speaking tour through Massachusetts and Vermont. Meetings were held in Johnson's hometown of Peacham, and they were guests of his brother Leonard Johnson. On a train ride from Barnet to White River Junction, Vermont, Garrison and Johnson were recognized by two passengers who were defending the Civil War (which had been in full swing for a year and half). They turned their attention to Garrison and Johnson, insulting them for being abolitionists. After a long string of derogatory comments and insults, another passenger defended the abolitionists and prevented a physical altercation.

The abolitionist lecturers experienced mixed receptions. There are always two sides to the coin, and there was support for abolitionists on the lecture circuit. Not every abolitionist event was met with angry mobs breaking down the doors. As the abolitionists spread their mission, many Vermonters were educated and changed their views of abolitionists.

Frederick Douglass wrote in *Life and Times of Frederick Douglass, Written by Himself* about the terrible reception he received in Middlebury, Vermont, but he also said, "In the neighboring town of Ferrisburgh the case was different and more favorable. The way had been prepared for us by such stalwart anti-slavery workers as Orson S. Murray, Charles C. Burleigh, Rowland T. Robinson and others."

William Wells Brown, fugitive slave abolitionist lecturer, traveled the Vermont circuit in 1860. Brown was born into slavery in Kentucky and escaped to Ohio at age twenty. He and his freed black wife moved to Buffalo, New York, and he was part of the Underground Railroad. After the 1850 Fugitive Slave Law passed, Brown chose to live in England for several years to avoid capture. Fortunately, a British couple bought Brown outright and gave him his freedom. In 1854, Brown and his family returned to the States so he could continue his work.

About his Vermont 1860 tour, Brown considered his trip to be worthwhile. In Garrison's *The Liberator*, Brown wrote on September 21, 1860, "Still, there are many warm hearts in the Green Mountain State, who are anxious to have the American Anti-Slavery Society send an agent or two, to lecture in all the towns. Vermont is certainly a good field for missionary labor." It is an interesting perspective to consider Vermont a mission field for abolitionism conversion, considering that Vermont was the first state to abolish slavery. But it shows that Vermont was like the other Northern states.

The flipside of that coin was apparent on another occasion when Brown stayed in Topsham in the Reverend N.R. Johnston's home. The Topsham Presbyterian Church hosted Brown's lecture, and the next morning, Johnston found a sign on his door that read, "Death to Traitors and Nigger Preachers!" Johnston also received death threats because of his abolitionist preaching and organizing lectures to Vermont towns.

Mobocracy occurred in every Northern state. The newspapers were filled with reports of mobs all over the North, and Vermont was no different. The following incidences were not rowdy teenagers but groups of law-abiding, taxpaying citizens. They were doctors, merchants, lawyers, farmers and bankers. They didn't want abolitionists to spread their "diseased" radical ideas.

If you were sitting in the town hall at a lecture and some angry people starting yelling and throwing things, it would be disruptive and distracting. A "mob" doesn't always mean hundreds of people; it could be a small number like six or more. Even six yelling and throwing things would be frightening. Just picture being at a lecture with people outside hurling bricks, breaking windows, throwing stones, firing cannons at buildings, smashing eggs and yelling—the violence was real.

Vermont historian of the nineteenth century Abigail Hemenway aptly described Vermont and the tension that existed during the antebellum period:

> *From 1832 to 1840, lectures against slavery met with an unwelcome reception in many towns in New England. Public sentiment was manifested on this subject by the people of Brattleboro, in the summer of 1837, was more suited to the atmosphere of Hartford, Connecticut or Charleston, South Carolina, than to the free air of Vermont. Looking back 40 years in our history and realizing the comparatively isolated condition and quiet avocations of the people, it is hard to account for the diseased state of the public mind as then exhibited upon this subject.*

OUTRAGE!

Fellow Citizens,

AN

ABOLITIONIST,

of the most revolting character is among you,
exciting the feelings of the North against the South.
A seditious Lecture is to be delivered

THIS EVENING,

at 7 o'clock, at the Presbyterian Church in
Cannon-street. You are requested to attend and unite in
putting down and silencing by peaceable means this tool
of evil and fanaticism. Let the rights of the States
guaranteed by the Constitution *be protected.*

Feb. 27, 1837. *The Union forever!*

Newspaper advertisements and anti-abolitionist handbills like this rendition of an "Outrage" ad ran in a February 27, 1837 newspaper, warning townspeople that an abolitionist would be lecturing and to join forces to stop the event. *Courtesy of Michelle Arnosky Sherburne.*

The United States in the 1830s was appropriately described as under "the reign of terror" by black historian and abolitionist William C. Nell because of the violence and increased pressure of the abolitionist movement.

Examples of Vermont mobocracy:

- *Abby Hemenway's Vermont: Unique Portrait of a State* stated that the Reverend E.R. Tyler of Brattleboro was lecturing on abolition in 1837, but the subject irritated a faction of residents who showed up at the lecture. While Tyler spoke, the antagonists set up a cannon and fired at the windows numerous times. He was threatened with a "tar and feathering." One of the Brattleboro residents reportedly stated they "should blow the Abolitionist down the bank!" Tyler wasn't a visitor; he was the minister in town.

- The *New Hampshire Patriot and State Gazette* of October 12, 1835, related an incident in Bradford, Vermont, in September 1835. An abolitionist was scheduled to speak at the Bradford Town Hall, but before the event, he was informed "his program was against the wishes of the people of the village to have the subject agitated." That did not discourage him, and the lecture was held that night. A group of men drove the fire department water wagon to the front of the building and rolled the fire hose to the front doors. While the lecturer spoke, the men blasted him with water. After a thorough drenching, the speaker gave up and left.

- The *Herald of Freedom* of November 14 and 28, 1835, reported that a month later and in a town north of Bradford, the Reverend George Storrs, a Vermont minister associated with the New Hampshire Anti-Slavery Society, was the guest speaker at the Newbury Seminary in Newbury Village. During Storrs's lecture, some individuals threw rocks at the front of the building and then entered heckling and threatening Storrs. The local authorities were called in and the perpetrators arrested. At their court hearing, Judge Jacob Collamer charged them with impeding Storrs's constitutional right to freedom of speech and fined them. It was reported that Collamer declared he could not "countenance abridgment of freedom of speech even if the disruption of the Union was being plotted," by abolitionists.

- *Freedom and Unity: A History of Vermont*, by the Vermont Historical Society, explained that abolitionist lecturers Oliver Johnson and Orson Murray received a bad reception at Middlebury College with students scraping their feet, showering the room with corn kernels and making all of kinds of disturbances to break up their meeting.

- The 1835 May riot in Montpelier is notorious for poor treatment of abolitionists in Vermont and is mentioned in numerous scholarly references. The Reverend Samuel May, a Connecticut abolitionist and Underground Railroad agent, was invited to conduct a lecture series in Montpelier by the Vermont Antislavery Society and Vermont legislature in October 1835. But forty civic leaders opposed the series. They stationed themselves outside the building, throwing eggs and stones at the windows while May spoke. Upon his departure, the mob harassed May, but a Quaker woman escorted May through the throng. The crowd would not harm him in the presence of a lady. The next day, May received a threatening letter from prominent Montpelier proslavery men advising him to leave town. Placards were set up around the church warning people not to attend, but May held his lecture anyway. As

May began his speech, threats from the crowd followed and women were asked to leave. The mob rushed toward May but was stopped by Colonel Jonathan Miller, a Montpelier abolitionist and Underground Railroad agent. Miller shouted and threatened them with bodily harm. They knew Miller was a veteran of the Greek wars, and they dispersed.

EVEN AS LATE as 1863, people didn't want to hear abolitionists' views. In Stowe, only an hour from Canada, the local Unitarian minister ran into opposition when he expressed his views on the new Emancipation Proclamation. During the Reverend H.P. Cutting's sermons about slavery and abolition, parishioners left during the service. A faction of the membership demanded Cutting's dismissal, but he had a larger number of supporters who outvoted them. The opponents formed their own church but wanted to use the same building.

Hemenway reported that Cutting and choir members were surprised one night to find the meetinghouse doors barricaded and windows nailed shut. When the choir group tried to get into the building, several people came out with clubs and bludgeons. A fight ensued, and Cutting's forces were able hold them off and then threatened to call the sheriff and the mob dispersed. They had to break down the door to get inside, but choir practice was eventually held.

The angry opponents later received orders from the sheriff to take possession of the parsonage and meetinghouse, and Cutting had to vacate the premises. Cutting refused to leave town and held "his church" in the old town hall until he could get legal use of the meetinghouse. Eventually, things simmered down and the opponents formed their own church and left Cutting alone. But in 1864, Cutting left Stowe for a pastorate in Minnesota.

Chapter 3

FEAR AND RISK FOR FUGITIVE SLAVES AND FREE BLACKS

Danger for fugitive slaves in the United States existed in many forms, like pursuit, capture and recognition. Fugitive slaves were afraid their whole lives, not just en route to their final destinations.

For free blacks—whether free born, legally manumitted or purchased—there was fear because they didn't have legal rights, were not considered equal citizens, and they were afraid of false accusations, persecution and of being kidnapped and sold into slavery.

There was no real freedom within America's borders as long as slavery existed. So why did fugitive slaves choose to stay in this country? For some, it was frightening to think of leaving the United States to live in another country, such as Canada. Many times, they had family members still in slavery, so staying in the States would make it possible to try to help them escape. Fugitives sometimes decided that the extra-long trip to Canada would be difficult, and they felt that if they could settle somewhere in the North with some support, it would be good enough.

In America, the laws favored slave owners and their rights. By law, a free black was unsafe to stay in Virginia for more than a month because he or she would automatically become a slave. Free blacks were not allowed to cross Tennessee or Virginia state lines. Black sailors were imprisoned in South Carolina if they came into port. While free blacks never felt truly safe, it was their neighbors, selectmen and customers who were the threat and not necessarily law enforcement, bounty hunters or angry slave owners.

In 1845, Frederick Douglass wrote about his fear in his first autobiography, *Narrative of the Life of Frederick Douglass*:

I was afraid to speak to anyone for fear of speaking to the wrong one and thereby falling into the hands of money-loving kidnappers...Trust No Man! I saw in every white man an enemy, and in almost every colored man cause for distrust. It was a most painful situation; and to understand it, one must needs experience it, or imagine himself in similar circumstances. Let him be a fugitive slave in a strange land...a land given up to be hunting ground for slaveholders—whose inhabitants are legalized kidnappers— where he is every moment subjected to the terrible liability of being seized upon by his fellowmen.

There were many fugitives who settled in Vermont who lived in fear, such as Cyrus Branch, alias "John White," in Manchester. White was a runaway Virginia slave who was pursued and went into hiding for eight years before working his way north. Once he settled in Manchester, he kept his slave status a secret because he was afraid of being returned to slavery. It wasn't until the Emancipation Proclamation that he shared his story with friends and neighbors.

Fugitive slave Ephraim Wright ended up at Noah Safford's safe house in Springfield and chose to settle there. He married another fugitive slave, raised a family and owned his own home. Locals said he was afraid of being recognized and worried about recapture. Wright was known for looking over his shoulder and not trusting newcomers. A story shared by Safford's daughter Rebecca Safford Holmes in the Springfield town history recounted that one day Wright was at the store and was sure he had seen his former master. He rushed to Safford's house and asked to be hidden until the coast was clear.

In 1843, St. Albans Underground Railroad agent Lawrence Brainerd helped Jeremiah C. Boggs, a Virginia runaway slave. Thirty-year-old Boggs traveled to Vermont because his brother was living in Montpelier. He chose to stay and was known as a hard and faithful worker. Brainerd's son Ezra told Wilbur Siebert in 1895 that Boggs learned to read and write while living in St. Albans.

But a year later, he was recognized by a St. Albans resident who was acquainted with Boggs's former master. Boggs got "running" fever and was afraid of being returned to slavery. Fortunately, an American Colonization Society recruiter was in town, persuading blacks to move to Liberia, where

Lawrence Brainerd was a well-known Underground Railroad agent in St. Albans, and he hid fugitive slaves in his home, pictured here. *Courtesy of the St. Albans Historical Society & Museum.*

they could be free. Boggs left for Liberia and a new life. The Brainerds received a letter from Boggs of his safe arrival.

Burlington Underground Railroad operator Lucius Bigelow had helped a fugitive slave who settled in Burlington. He bought a house, had a family and worked as a waiter at a restaurant beside the railroad station. The man was working one day and saw his former owner in the restaurant and left immediately. He went to Bigelow, who put him on the train to Canada. Then Bigelow notified the man's wife and family of his whereabouts. He arranged for them to join him in Canada.

RECAPTURE HAPPENED ALL over the country, and fugitive slaves were returned to their owners. There was no statute of limitations. A Maryland slave, the Reverend Alexander Helmsley escaped to New Jersey, and eight years later, he was turned into the authorities as a fugitive. Friends brought his case to the New Jersey Supreme Court, and in a rare case, Helmsley won and was freed. He fled to Canada and lived the rest of his life there. Helmsley stated in an 1854 interview: "For some ten years, I was in hopes that something might happen, whereby I might return to my old home in New Jersey. I watched the newspapers and they told the story. I found that there would be risk in going back—and that was confirmed by many of my fellow men falling into the same catastrophe that I did—the same things happen now."

Free blacks could be sent into slavery unjustly, and trying to prove their "free" status was extremely difficult as blacks had no rights. There were plenty of bounty hunters and people looking to make easy money who preyed on unsuspecting blacks. They could run a scam operation and deceive authorities that a person was a runaway.

"Even Negroes who were legally free were often made victims of a device commonly used by agents of slave hunters. This was to send South exact descriptions of Negroes living in the North whom it was intended to kidnap. The descriptions were printed as handbills to be displayed as proof of ownership when the alleged fugitive was seized and brought before a magistrate. All too often magistrates found such evidence convincing," wrote William Breyfogle in *Make Free; The Story of the Underground Railroad.*

All it would take was one white person to point out a black person and say, "I think I know this is a fugitive," and the shackles were on, no questions asked, and the black person was shipped to the slave auction. Similarly, if a black person made a white person angry, he could be turned in, whether he was a fugitive or free.

A story of trickery is in *Norwich, Vermont: A History* about Norwich native Jim Glory. Glory was a free black man who served in the War of 1812. After the war, he worked for a mule driver who transported mules to Southern states to sell. Glory accompanied the driver often. But the story goes that on one trip, the mule driver and Glory planned a scam. The mule driver would sell Glory as slave, then Glory would escape and they would meet up and split the money. Apparently, the sale of Glory occurred, but the scam was on him. The mule driver deserted Glory and kept all the money. Glory ended up a slave for life.

Tricked, kidnapped and sold into slavery was Solomon Northup in Saratoga Springs, New York. Northup had connections to Vermont because he traveled the state on the lecture circuit after his slavery experience. On numerous occasions, he helped Hartland, Vermont agent Lame John Smith transport fugitive slaves to the next safe house.

Northup was born a free black in upstate New York. He was a musician and had a family and a home. In 1841, two swindlers came to town and convinced him of a job opportunity in Washington, D.C. Luring him to D.C., he was drugged, kidnapped and thrown into a slave pen for sale. He was sold into slavery and sent to the South for twelve years. Once the chains were on, Northup couldn't do anything to prove he wasn't a slave. His wife enlisted help from the New York governor. It took twelve years to get through the red tape, but they were able to get Northup freed. Northup spent the rest of his life as an abolitionist lecturer, and he wrote his autobiography and helped fugitive slaves to freedom.

FUGITIVE SLAVES AND PURSUIT

One of the earliest Vermont incidences of an attempted recapture of a fugitive slave was reported by eyewitness Horace Greeley, who was an apprentice at a Vermont newspaper in East Poultney in 1830.

A fugitive slave had escaped from his New York owner and landed in East Poultney. He decided to stay. His master conducted a search for him and learned of his whereabouts. When the master arrived in town and tried to reclaim the slave, the townspeople gathered on the village green and protected the fugitive. The slave owner was forced to leave empty-handed. Greeley, the reporter, was influenced by that event and became an abolitionist who established the *New York Tribune* and was its editor for over thirty years.

It has been recorded that bounty hunters traveled as far north as Burlington in search of a mark if they had a definite lead and the money was worth it. Famous Vermont Underground Railroad agent Rowland T. Robinson wrote about Samuel Chalker in Vergennes serving as the "slave catcher lookout." Chalker alerted Burlington Underground Railroad agents Lucius Bigelow and the Reverend Joshua Young when he spotted suspicious characters in his town. Bigelow and Young were often targets of stakeouts when a fugitive deal was underway.

Across the Vermont eastern border in Lyme, New Hampshire, the Samuel Balch home was an Underground Railroad safe house that has been in the Balch family since the nineteenth century. Lyme Underground Railroad agents had heavy fugitive slave traffic because of its promixity to Canaan, New Hampshire and the active Underground Railroad agents there. Once a month, fugitives were taken from Canaan to Lyme and then across the Connecticut River into Vermont towns.

In a 1992 newspaper interview, Samuel's great-grandson Charles Balch shared a story of Samuel helping slaves:

One night, a group of fugitive slaves arrived at Balch's home. There was urgency to hide them because the Balchs had received word that federal agents were in pursuit. Samuel quickly hid them, and his wife separated one, petite elderly woman and hid her upstairs in bed with the Balch children.

As expected, the authorities showed up at his house and accused Samuel of illegal conduct. Samuel allowed them to search the house. When they headed for the bedrooms upstairs, Mrs. Balch warned them not to wake the children. The agents opened the bedroom door, and all they saw were children sleeping tucked under quilts. Not finding any fugitives, the agents left the Balch house. Tucked under the covers and out of sight was the slave woman. Mrs. Balch's plan worked, and when it was safe, Samuel loaded up his stowaways in his wagon and took them to Bliss Tavern in Haverhill, New Hampshire.

In the *Boardman Genealogy, 1525–1895,* Norwich resident Stephen Carver Boardman's Underground Railroad work was recorded. Boardman and his wife aided fugitive slaves, and they used aliases to protect their identities with their Underground Railroad connections and fugitive slaves. A story of pursuit was passed on by Stephen's son, Charles, who was thirteen at the time and helped his father in the venture.

A fugitive family of three arrived at the family's home. They were being pursued by a bounty hunter. Boardman had them wet their shoes in camphor to throw the bloodhounds off their scent and hid them to a cellar out in his cornfield.

The bounty hunter arrived at Boardman's house with a U.S. marshal and deputies with bloodhounds to search the premises for slaves. Boardman turned them away because they didn't have a warrant. The authorities left to get one.

Boardman and Charles got the family from the cellar. Boardman hid them in his wagon and drove twenty-five miles to Randolph. He was able to leave them in the care of a fellow Underground Railroad operator who worked the Central Vermont Railroad. The next stop was with a Montpelier agent, and they were taken to Canada.

While working their way out of slave states, another danger for fugitives were slave patrols. Slave patrols were police organizations affiliated with state militias, and their sole purpose was to travel the roads searching for runaway slaves.

Slave catching was more prevalent when the slaves had just fled their owners and slave catchers were hot on their trail. Slave owners advertised in the newspapers when a slave ran away, and they also hired slave catchers to retrieve their property.

False fugitive slave handbills were printed with descriptions of free blacks and used to arrest innocent free men and women. After 1850, professional slave catchers opened offices advertising their services to Southern slave owners.

Risk and danger for fugitives as well as the Underground Railroad agents increased after the Fugitive Slave Law of 1850 went into effect.

Before 1850, it was illegal to help a fugitive slave. As the migration westward increased in the mid-1800s, the North and South vied for every new state to get more leverage in Congress. The Southern states were tired of the North pressuring them about slavery. Finally the Fugitive Slave Law of 1850 was passed to appease the South, but it infuriated the Northerners. The law required every U.S. citizen to turn in fugitive slaves.

As a form of defiance, many Northerners chose to ignore the law, and it is difficult to find court cases or newspaper accounts of fugitive slave returns after 1850. Throughout the nation, there was increased activity of the Underground Railroad instead of people abiding by the new law and turning in fugitives. The law fueled abolitionists to do as much as they could to help fugitive slaves.

Another ripple effect from this law was that many records of Underground Railroad assistance were destroyed. Any paper trail linking a person to helping a fugitive, or even an affiliation to an antislavery society, was destroyed. Documented proof of aiding fugitives was incriminating and dangerous.

In His Own Words:
John White Living Incognito in Vermont

John White lived in Manchester for twenty-nine years and no one knew his past or his real name. He lived, married, worked and was accepted into the community. But White had a secret: he was a fugitive slave. It wasn't until after the Civil War and the Emancipation Proclamation that he decided he could share his secret.

He had been born a slave in Petersburg, Virginia, and was owned by the same master for thirty years until the master died. His slave name was Cyrus Branch, and he was sold four times, ending up in City Point, Virginia. He tried to buy his freedom through manumission, but because of his carpentry skills, his master refused. White's wife and children were sold to a neighboring slave owner, and White's owner refused to let him visit them.

That was the final straw, and White decided he would not spend another day in slavery. It meant leaving his wife and children. He escaped and headed northeast to Bermuda Hundred, where he had once lived and where his parents, who were slaves, were living. He got to Martyr's Swamp near the James River and lived in the swamp.

But he was still in Virginia, a slave state. A duck hunter spotted him and wanted the bounty. White was shot with birdshot several times but crawled to a hiding spot. He dragged himself to his parents' place and had to be hidden and nursed back to health.

When he was able, his father sent him to another swamp to hide in. So for another four years, White made his home there, catching fish and selling it to boatmen for bread and meat.

It was a lonely existence, and he received help from local slaves. White was discovered again, pursued by dogs and shot at. Some sailor friends hid him on a boat that was headed north. He was ready to get out of Virginia. He traveled up the Hudson River and was helped by two pastors, who transported him to Troy and Hoosick Falls, New York, and then to Shaftsbury, Vermont.

He stayed in hiding in Shaftsbury for two months before the agent sent him to Manchester to Judge John Pettibone's home in 1840.

Once he was in Manchester, White decided it was safe to stop running. He used an alias, John White, and got a job, married and had a new family. It was a new life, but he didn't tell anyone about his past. Pettibone and another agent, Daniel Roberts, knew White had come through the Underground Railroad, and two men respected his secret.

White became active in the church, serving as the sexton. He was a handyman, doing jobs like gardening, housecleaning, fixing stoves, cleaning carpets and whitewashing fences. He helped at the polls as a ticket distributor and was a staunch Republican.

In the 1850 U.S. Federal Census records, under "Free Inhabitants in Manchester, VT, County of Bennington, VT, October 16, 1850" John White is recorded as a forty-eight-year-old black man born in Virginia. He is listed as a property owner of $400 worth of real estate. His second wife was Polly, and in 1850, he had two daughters, ages sixteen and six. Looking through the 1860 Census records for Manchester, there were only three other black families in town.

Not until after the Emancipation Proclamation did White decide he could pursue finding his lost family. He asked a Manchester resident who was traveling to Virginia to ask around for any relatives of a "Cyrus Branch."

Cyrus Branch, alias "John White" is recorded in the 1860 U.S. Federal Population Census Record as living in Manchester, Bennington County, Vermont. He is listed as head of household, a black male, sixty-seven years old at the time of the census, with the birth year of 1793 in Virginia. Living in his household is his wife, Polly, fifty-six, and daughter Mary, sixteen. *Courtesy of FamilySearch.org, source, National Archives.*

The query was successful, and two long-lost daughters of Cyrus Branch were found. White began corresponding with his daughters and learned what had happened to his family. His first wife had passed away a few years before. But his family had been found!

At age seventy-five, White decided to share his slave background with his Manchester friends. They encouraged him to share his story and go visit his family.

Manchester resident Elizabeth Wickham was a member of the same church as White and volunteered to write an article about his life. She wrote an article that was published in the *Manchester Journal* on January 12, 1869. A month later, it was printed as a pamphlet called, "A Lost Family Found: An Authentic Narrative of Cyrus Branch and His Family, Alias John White, of Manchester, Vermont" to raise money for a trip to Virginia to see his family.

It is interesting that in his narrative, he did not give the names of the men who assisted him. White was afraid to identify Underground Railroad agents in New York and Vermont because he felt there were still lingering security issues. They could receive retribution or backlash if their part in the

Underground Railroad was known. He eventually traveled to Petersburg, Virginia, and was reunited with his daughters.

Wickham wrote: "What happier event could transpire, or imagination devise, than that Cyrus Branch, alias, John White, after 33 years of absence from kindred, and in ignorance concerning them, and amid the most depressing circumstances on both sides, should meet a sister, and sister's children, his own children, and the grand-children unknown to him, and they, together be permitted to recount the mercies of the Lord, in their thus beholding each other's face in the land of the living; and in the very State where they were in bondage, but in which, through the wonderful Providence of God, ALL now are free."

PREJUDICE AND RACISM

Prejudice and racism was as prevalent in the Green Mountain state as in any other state. Antislavery did not mean non-racist. In John Lovejoy's "Racism in Antebellum Vermont" essay in the *Vermont History Journal*, he wrote, "Still, Vermonters' participation in antiabolition mobs indicates the active presence in the state of a virulent form of racism."

Freedom may have been given to blacks in Northern states, but with that came poverty. Finding steady work was an issue. Blacks did not work in mills, factories or lumberyards. Competition for low-paying jobs was between poor whites and immigrants, leaving out the blacks.

Andrew Harris, the first black University of Vermont graduate, said in an 1839 lecture about racism, "If he wishes to be useful as a professional man, a merchant or mechanic, he is prevented by the color of his skin, and driven to those menial employments which tend to bring us more and more into disrepute."

The North has tried to ignore the reality that racism and prejudice existed in its boundaries. Joanne Pope Melish, author of *Disowning Slavery: Gradual Emancipation and "Race" in New England, 1780-1860* hit the mark with the Northern attitude about slavery. Melish wrote, "The absolute amnesia about slavery here on the one hand, and the gradualness of slavery ending on the other, work together to make race a very distinctive thing in New England. If you have obliterated the historical memory of actual slavery—because we're the free states, right?—that makes it possible to turn around and look at a population that is disproportionately poor and say, it must be their own inferiority. That is where New England's particular brand of racism comes from."

Charles McKay was a Scottish writer who toured the United States and Canada during the Antebellum period, writing *Life and Liberty in America; or Sketches of a Tour in the United States and Canada in 1857–58*. His observances of the Northern citizens' treatment of blacks give a temperature reading of the American atmosphere. McKay aptly called it "the language of the free North":

> *We shall not make the black man a slave; we shall not buy him or sell him; but we shall not associate with him. He shall be free to live and to thrive, if he can, and to pay taxes and perform duties; But he shall not be free to dine and drink at our board—To mingle with us in the concert-room, the lecture-room, the theatre or the church, or to marry with our daughters. We are of another race, and he is inferior. Let him know his place—and keep it.*

In the early 1800s, anthropology and craniology theories used science to discriminate against blacks. Even in the antislavery state of Vermont, Middlebury College, University of Vermont and Norwich University offered these courses, as did Dartmouth College in Hanover, New Hampshire. Then it was the height of hypocrisy for these same colleges to admit black students.

"By the 1830s, 'colorphobia' was so ubiquitous that even white antislavery people believed in the inferiority of blacks because of the 'scientific racism' of the day," Elise Guyette stated in *Blacks in Vermont*.

Middlebury College is an example of Vermont's ever-swinging pendulum of tolerance and acceptance. Middlebury offered racial inferiority courses and yet graduated Alexander Twilight in 1823, the first African American to graduate in the U.S. It also gave black pastor Lemuel Haynes an honorary degree in 1804.

Middlebury College was inconsistent when accepting students as well. The college denied a black man, Andrew Harris, admission in 1837 because of his race but in 1845 allowed Rutland black native Martin Freeman to attend.

An example of prejudice occurred in Newbury, Vermont, the same town where an 1835 abolitionist lecture was stopped by a mob. Ten years later, the Newbury Seminary had over three hundred students and a stellar reputation that attracted students from all over the country. In 1842, a black girl applied for admission, and the locals were against it. The public consensus was that teaching blacks to read and write was wrong. The seminary administration wavered on allowing her admission.

Upon the insistence of teacher Rachel Smith, the administration allowed her to stay under the condition that she was the responsibility of Smith. Many were disgusted and predicted the school's ruin because of this decision. *History of the Town of Newbury* stated, "Her coming made some sensation…We can hardly comprehend in these days a state of affairs which make this act, one of moral heroism."

Life wasn't easy for blacks living in Vermont. In rural communities, it may have been even harder for them. Not living in town, a neighbor could harass you and no one would know about it. Even if you brought in the authorities, the neighbor would stop for a while but resume.

The experiences of the Prince family from 1760s to 1820s were fraught with persecution and difficulty. They were never left alone by white neighbors. It was a rough life for people who were supposed to be free.

Lucy Terry, born in Africa and kidnapped for the slave trade, lived in Massachusetts. She was the first African American female poet who immortalized the 1746 Native American attack on a section of Deerfield, Massachusetts, called "The Bars" in the ballad "Bars Fight."

Lucy's freedom was purchased by a free black man, Abijah Prince, who then married her in 1756. Lucy and Abijah moved to Guilford, Vermont, in the 1760s and had six children. They owned a farm, but soon after moving in, white neighbors began harassing the Princes, damaging their property and setting livestock loose and assaulting their sons.

They were the targets of one neighbor who hired a group of men to attack them and run them off their own property. The Princes were in and out of court, suing these neighbors. In 1785, Lucy went to the Vermont governor and pleaded their case. She posed a convincing argument to the governor, explaining the multiple offenses by two specific neighbors. The governor ruled in the Princes' favor, which was a landmark ruling but had little bearing back in Guilford. The abuses continued.

Abijah died and the Prince family moved to Sunderland. But the scene didn't change, and Lucy was always fighting to be left alone. She lived to be one hundred, dying in 1821. Her "Bars Fight" poem was published thirty years after her death.

As long as there were blacks living in the United States, they were segregated and denied equal treatment, even if they were proven free men and women. While traveling, they were not allowed to ride in the stagecoaches or below deck, and hotels and restaurants refused to serve them.

In 1847, former fugitive slaves Lewis and Harriet Hayden of Boston, Massachusetts, were segregated from white passengers on the steamboat from Whitehall, New York, to Vergennes for a reunion with Delia Webster, the Vermont native responsible for their freedom.

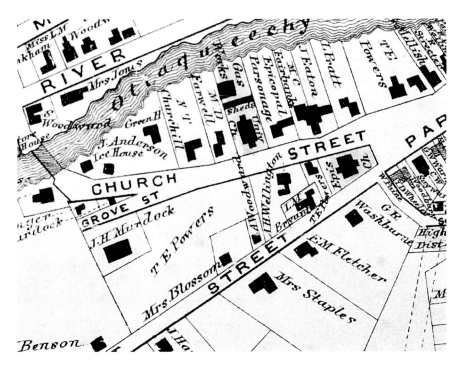

This close-up of the 1856 Woodstock map shows property owned by Dr. Thomas E. Powers on Church Street in Woodstock. In the 1830s, Powers lived in the house labeled "M.D. Farwell" beside the Universalist chapel. The apartment house where black people lived for about fifteen years before they were forced to leave was located in the "T.E. Powers" building behind the "Epis. Church" on this map. *Courtesy of the Woodstock Historical Society, Inc. Map of Windsor County, VT 1856, Woodstock, by Hosea Doton in their collection. Photo by Michelle Arnosky Sherburne.*

In South Woodstock in 1820, black families moved into apartment houses near the Universalist Chapel at the southern end of the Woodstock Green. They were welcomed at first. As time went on and national tension permeated every town, South Woodstock residents decided they didn't want blacks there. Prejudice and snobbery replaced hospitality and friendliness. Even after fifteen years of them living there, it wasn't acceptable to have blacks living in town.

In 1835, it was reported that forty men showed up at the apartment house one night armed with torches, clubs, axes, chains, ropes and oxen. It was a frightening, violent scene. Windows were smashed, doors were axed and they forced their way in. The families fled from the apartment house to Powers, an Underground Railroad agent. The black families were taken out of town and never seen again.

IN HIS OWN WORDS: JEFFREY BRACE

"I underwent many difficulties…being among strangers who felt but little kindness for people of my color," wrote Jeffrey Brace. Brace lived in Vermont as a free black for forty-three years, residing in the towns of Poultney, Manchester, Shelton and Georgia. Only in Georgia were Brace and his family treated fairly. His Vermont experience spanned from 1784 to 1827, before the abolitionist movement and right after Vermont's abolishing of slavery.

"I have concluded it my duty to myself, to all Africans who can read, to the Church, in short to all mankind, to thus publish these my memoirs, that all may see how poor Africans have been and perhaps now are abused by a christian and enlightened people…it is my anxious wish that this simple narrative may be the means of opening the hearts of those who hold slaves and move them to consent to give them that freedom which they themselves enjoy, and which all mankind have an equal right to possess," Brace wrote. Brace wrote his memoir, *The Blind African, or Memoirs of Boyrereau Brinch, Nick-named Jeffrey Brace*, in 1810 and told his story.

Born in West Africa in 1742, Brace was kidnapped as a teenager and brought to America. He spent most of his life as a slave in Connecticut. He fought in the Revolutionary War and was given his freedom for his military service.

At forty-two years old, he chose to begin a new life in Vermont because he had heard good things about the state. However, things were not what they seemed, and Brace encountered prejudice.

He married Susannah, a former African slave who was a single mother. Brace worked for himself, but he ran into difficulties. He would complete a job and not get paid or have work lined up but be dismissed after a few days. He eventually purchased twenty-five acres in Poultney and built a log house for his family.

Unfortunately, he could not find work in the area, so the family moved to Manchester. Persecution began just as the family settled in.

They were shocked to received news from the Manchester selectmen that Susannah's twelve-year-old son would be taken from the family and made an indentured servant, with no parental permission necessary. The authorities didn't think blacks were capable of raising their own children. Brace fought the selectmen, but the boy was taken anyway.

When Susannah and Jeffrey had a daughter, arrangements were made at her birth by Manchester selectmen that the girl would be an indentured servant as soon as she was old enough. Brace tried to take legal action at various times in his life but to no avail.

The Brace family moved back to their Poultney property, possibly to get away from the Manchester persecution. But no matter where they went, they suffered oppression, prejudice, injustice and persecution. Brace had numerous legal disputes with neighbors through the years, only winning one dispute.

In Poultney, the Braces' neighbor antagonized the family with property line disputes, property damage and damage to livestock. Susannah was even assaulted by the neighbor man during a fight. Whenever there was a conflict, the neighbor complained to the select board, which in turn threatened to take the Brace children away.

For seven years, the Braces were persecuted by the neighbor with endless battles and finally decided to leave. They sold the land and moved to Sheldon, 114 miles north. But even there, the Brace family received a cold reception. Brace attempted to purchase fifty acres and began to clear the land, but the property was sold to a white man. Soon Brace was told by town officials that he and his family had to leave town.

In 1804, the Braces moved to Georgia, Vermont, and the Braces finally found a quiet place to live. They were allowed to live in peace, and Jeffrey and a son-in-law purchased sixty acres. Jeffrey and Susannah joined the Baptist church in nearby Swanton. Susannah died in 1807.

Jeffrey was well known in Georgia as a well-respected abolitionist. He went blind, but that didn't stop him from publishing his autobiography in 1810. *The Blind African Slave* was well written, with detailed descriptions of his native country, its resources, nature, people, culture and customs. Unlike many slave narratives of that period, Brace focused on information about his life in Africa.

It took three years for Brace to receive a pension for his Revolutionary War service. In 1821, he finally got paid from the government. At eighty-five, he died in 1827, a respected, honorable man, despite all the hardships that he endured.

NOYES ACADEMY:
A TOXIC MIX OF HATRED, PREJUDICE AND RACISM

Thirteen miles east of Thetford, Vermont, over the New Hampshire border is Canaan, New Hampshire. During the Underground Railroad years, Canaan had a steady flow of fugitive slave traffic coming north from Concord, New Hampshire, and Canaan agents sent them through Lyme and into Vermont at Thetford and Post Mills. In the early 1830s, Canaan abolitionists established Noyes Academy, a school for blacks and whites, but it became a tragedy known

The *Destruction of Noyes Academy* was painted by Mikel Wells in 1999 commissioned by the Canaan Historical Society. It depicts the 1835 mob scene of the Noyes Academy building being dragged down the middle of Canaan's Main Street. The school was destroyed, and the black students escaped on the Underground Railroad. *Courtesy of painter Mikel Wells, 1999, owned by Canaan Historical Society, digital image from* Upper Valley Life *magazine, September/October 2008 issue.*

far and wide in the United States. It was an example of how intolerance, prejudice and ignorance rose to extreme levels and destroyed something good.

Canaan abolitionists received a charter from the New Hampshire legislature in July 1834 to establish a school that would provide higher education for blacks and whites equally. There were sixty financial contributors, and land was purchased and a schoolhouse built south of the North Congregational Church. The main dormitory was the Furber-Harris House, owned by Underground Railroad agent John H. Harris.

The school opened March 1, 1835, with fourteen black students and twenty-eight white students. Black students came from New York City; Boston; Concord, New Hampshire; Providence, Rhode Island; and Hamilton, Massachusetts, and their trips were difficult due to prejudice and segregation. They were not allowed to stay in hotels, be served in restaurants or travel indoors in stagecoaches or on ships. Relieved to arrive in Canaan, the students began their education.

William Lloyd Garrison's *The Liberator* acknowledged the opening of Noyes Academy in its March 14, 1835 issue as an institution "for youth of good character, without distinction of color."

Noyes Academy put Canaan on the New England map, and in a short time, the school became notorious for allowing black students. The year 1835 was a tense one for abolitionists, described as the "reign of terror" for the intolerance blacks and abolitionists faced in the country. Local opponents of Noyes Academy were angered because they did not believe that blacks should be educated. Canaan got a bad reputation for promoting education for blacks, and some residents were afraid that the school would draw a huge population of blacks who would overrun the town.

Not all Canaanites were opposed to the school. But Canaan resident Jacob Trussell rallied support from area New Hampshire towns such as Enfield, Hanover and Dorchester to fight the academy. He held meetings during the spring. Trussell held a special town meeting with no academy representatives or supporters present. In the *History of Canaan, NH,* it was reported that a resolution was passed that stated: "Resolved, that we view the abhorrence the attempt of the Abolitionists to establish a school in this town, for the instruction of the sable sons and daughters of Africanus, in common with our own sons and daughters and that we view with contempt every white man and woman who may have pledged themselves to receive black boarders."

After only four months, the Noyes Academy was doomed.

On July 4, 1835, Trussell and his gang tried to take over the school, carrying clubs and shouting threats. The local magistrate and school supporter Dr. Timothy Tilton was able to scare them off by shouting warnings and threatening to arrest them.

Meetings were held on July 11 and 31 about legally removing the school, and no town officials attempted to stop the process. A date was set to remove the building and force the closure of Noyes Academy. Canaan residents who weren't involved were afraid of the academy opponents. The fate of the students hung in the balance.

The Great Hauling

Early August 10, 1835, Canaan's Main Street was cluttered with seventy men with wagons filled with iron bars, chains and axes and about ninety-five yoked oxen headed for Noyes Academy. Tilton tried to defend the academy, but this time, he was outnumbered and retreated.

The students feared for their lives. They watched the scene from their boardinghouses in terror. Canaan residents also watched the mob scene in fear. If they voiced any opposition, they were insulted and ridiculed.

Axes struck the walls and doors. Crowbars pried the building up, lifting and loosening it from its foundation. Chains were hooked around the base of the building, and the ox teams were attached. They worked in the afternoon heat until finally the building shifted and the teams pulled it off the foundation.

By 7:00 p.m., the mob had dragged the building into the middle of Main Street. That night, one of the troublemakers tried to set the building on fire, but it died out.

On August 11, the work crew assembled and continued their quest. Progress went quicker with cables instead of chains, dragging the building down the street. By noon, they stopped in front of the general store, demanding a barrel of rum. A storekeeper refused, but after much struggling, Trussell's men had the rum. One of the women who lived on Main Street harassed the mob as they went by. The storekeeper ordered her to get in her house.

It took all afternoon to drag the academy building to the corner of the common, right in front of the church. Trussell gave speeches and rallied the crowd. Trussell announced that the Noyes Academy students had one month to leave town, and if they didn't, they would be removed by force.

With the August heat, the mob stopped for the day and spent that night drinking, celebrating their triumph, antagonizing townspeople and threatening to attack the boardinghouses.

Henry Highland Garnet, later a famous abolitionist lecturer, was one of the black students and wrote about his experiences later in life. He wrote that the mob surrounded the house where he and other students were living. A shot was fired into the room where Garnet was. Garnet, in response, took a rifle and fired a shot to discourage the mob. He recalled that the students were split up and taken out of town by different Underground Railroad agents.

The building stayed in the middle of the street until September 11, when the selectmen ordered Trussell and a smaller crew to haul the building into a field. Trussell's crew celebrated the completion of the work with a parade of cannon, fifes and drums down Main Street. Trussell had cannons fired at all the abolitionists' houses.

Trussell ended the day with a farewell address, in which he heralded the work and efforts of fighting the "Abolition Monster, that ascended out of the bottomless pit, is sent headlong to perdition, and the mourners go about the streets."

The Noyes Academy was no more. It was a sad day in the history of Canaan known as the "Day of the Great Hauling." After the furor had died down, the town held meetings with regard to the Noyes Academy removal. People realized the gravity of what had happened and that it didn't improve Canaan's reputation. Trussell was reprimanded for his role in the destruction of the school, and in March 1836, he was excommunicated from the church. He left town.

As for the Noyes Academy building, it sat empty for three years until March 1839 when the building was set on fire. And the students? They found safer places to live and continued their education.

For example, Henry Highland Garnet, himself from a family of ex-slaves, became a minister and was involved in the temperance, abolitionist and colonization movements. He was a leading abolitionist, attending conventions all over the North. He was appointed as minister to Liberia, the colonizationist destination. He died there after a long life of fighting for the rights of blacks.

Chapter 4
BLACKS IN VERMONT

As with any Northern state in the United States from 1800 to 1863, there were free blacks living and working in Vermont. Frederick Douglass, Harriet Tubman, William Still, Lewis Hayden, Booker T. Washington, Sojourner Truth and others lived in Northern states and accomplished great things despite inequality and racism.

Vermont had a small population of blacks during this timeframe, according to census records and town histories—only seven hundred, according to the 1860 U.S. census. The black population was made up of fugitive slaves who chose to stay, native Vermonters and some who moved to the state and settled with their families. Blacks fared better if they were farmers or lived in isolated communities like "the Hill" in Hinesburgh, Vermont.

The Short History of Thetford, Vt. noted that "the total impression given by these scattered bits of evidence is that there was a small group of Blacks in town, living somewhat separately from the other inhabitants." In some rare cases, they were allowed to join churches, like Jeffrey Brace did in Georgia or Shubael Clark in Hinesburgh, or work in the church like John "Cyrus Branch" White in Manchester. In Woodstock and Reading, blacks were accepted in the community and were property owners.

There were eleven black families living on "the Hill" in Hinesburgh, separate from the rest of the town. Elise Guyette wrote *Discovering Black Vermont: African American Farmers in Hinesburgh, 1790–1890*, which dealt with the unique community of black families that did not experience the racial tension as badly as other blacks in Vermont, because of their self-sufficient, tight-knit unit.

Guyette's 1992 University of Vermont thesis was "The Working Lives of African Vermonters in Census and Literature, 1790-1870," and she compiled tables of the largest African American communities in Vermont over a period of eighty years. The table featured every ten years between 1790 and 1870. The towns with the highest black population during that period were: Burlington, with 71 in 1820; Rutland, with 67 in 1840; St. Albans, with 67 in 1850; and Rutland again, with 93 in 1860.

The numbers are clearly very low, with the black population at its largest in 1850 at only 1.2 percent of the population. For example, Manchester had only two black families living in town, according to the 1850 census. In some Vermont towns, blacks were recorded as living in white households.

In 1791, there were 157 households in Thetford with only two black families in town. An 1800 census recorded that there was only one black family living alone while the rest of the blacks lived in white households. In Norwich, there were ten free blacks living in white households, according to 1820 and 1830 census records. In the 1840 census, there was only one black family on record. By 1850, there were two separate households of blacks.

Woodstock was a community that allowed free blacks to live in its midst. It was recorded in the Vermont soldier rosters that eleven men served in the Massachusetts Regiment from the Woodstock community. The 1800s newspapers in town ran obituaries for blacks. In the 1790 Vermont Census, there were 58 free blacks. The 1872 *Walton's Farmer's Almanac* listed the "Free Colored" population of Windsor County as 110.

In the 1850 and 1860 U.S. Census for Springfield, fugitive slave Ephraim Wright is listed as head of household. He changed his census information because he was a fugitive. He changed the state he was born in from Maryland to Virginia, and he changed his race from "black" to "mulatto." Sometimes incorrect information was given to the census taker if a person was afraid of repercussions.

It was reported that approximately 150 African Americans from Vermont served in the Union army. The famous Fifty-fourth Massachusetts Regiment reported 68 Vermont African American recruits, and they hailed from all over the state: St. Albans, Castleton, Burlington, Woodstock, Hartland, Bennington, Windsor, Hinesburg, Rutland, Lincoln, Bristol, Monkton, Ferrisburgh, Bridgewater, Corinth, Fair Haven, Rockingham, Chittenden, West Fairlee, Pownal, Underhill, Charlotte and Vernon.

Brattleboro

A 1912 *Vermont Phoenix* newspaper article featured a resident Jake Cartlidge, who was referred to as "Brattleboro's only living ex-slave." The community interceded for Cartlidge to receive a government pension for his military service.

Jake was born into slavery in Georgia around 1837. As a young man, he was sold on the auction block to a harsh slave owner. He recalled severe beatings, and he decided he had had enough. He escaped and worked his way north, hiding out in fields and swamps. When he reached Pennsylvania, he joined a railroad crew of fellow blacks and stayed there a while. Then he was recruited into the Pennsylvania Regiment Company D in 1864. Jake fought in the Civil War and was discharged.

He traveled to New England and stopped in Rutland. After a year, he moved to Brattleboro and decided to stay. He was a jack-of-all-trades and worked for a local coal dealer. He shared his slave experiences with Brattleboro residents. He was seventy-five years old at the time of the article and moved to Chesterfield, New Hampshire, to live with friends until he died.

Thetford

In 1775, a black man named Prince Saunders lived in town. He went to Boston for his education. He taught at a black school and then moved to England, where he was accepted into the British social circles. From there, he became a confidential advisor to Emperor Christopher of Haiti. But he lost favor with the Haiti emperor and returned to the States for a while. After the emperor's death, Prince Saunders returned to Haiti in 1839 and became the attorney general there.

Hinesburgh: The Hill Community

In the late 1790s, two black families settled in Hinesburgh on Lincoln Hill, known locally as "the Hill." Shubael and Violet Clark bought land on the Hill and had nine children. Prince and Hannah Peters moved to the Hill in 1798 with four children.

As time went on, more black families settled there—the Moons, Langleys, Williams, Princes and Waters. The Hill families were landowners and prosperous farmers. They gradually were welcomed into the Hinesburgh community.

They didn't face the usual racial tension there. Elise Guyette wrote a comprehensive book on the subject, *Discovering Black Vermont*, and she stated that the black families on the Hill "created a safe space for themselves that they controlled, where they had found friends both black and white, and where relatives of three generations were living closely together in rural, middle-class style. This Hill in Hinesburgh was more than just a piece or ground; it had been baptized by their toil…To have such a place in America was something few liberated blacks could have achieved at the time."

In Guyette's research, the Baptist Church in Hinesburgh accepted these families into the church. Asa Moon and Shubael Clark even served as elders. They addressed issues of membership truancy. The Hill men were allowed to vote on town issues. The families participated in community activities, and the Hill children went to local schools.

Two Maryland fugitive slaves settled in Hinesburgh. One of them, Edward Williams, arrived in Hinesburgh in the late 1830s and married Phoebe, Shubael's daughter, in 1839.

William Langley, a black man from Pittsford, married Almira Clark, another of Shubael's daughters, in 1821. The Langleys had seven children, one of whom was Loudon Langley. William and Almira harbored fugitive slaves in their home on the Hill. Later, Loudon assisted fugitives himself as an adult, and he became an outspoken abolitionist.

Over time, the children moved away from the Hill, and the founding family members died. Bad economic times hit the Hill, and families lost their farms and ended up working as laborers on white farms. By the 1890s, the Hill community was no more.

WEST RUTLAND

Lemuel Haynes was born in 1756, the illegitimate child of a black man and a white woman, and was then adopted by a white Massachusettes family. He received an education and studied Latin, Greek and theology. When the Revolutionary War began, Haynes enlisted.

After the war, Haynes was licensed to preach in 1780. Haynes married a white Connecticut woman in 1783, and they had ten children. He moved his family to West Rutland in 1783 when he became pastor of an all-white congregation. He served for thirty years and was known as a dynamic preacher and was well-respected in the community. Middlebury College granted Haynes an honorary degree in 1804.

Times changed though, and racism crept in where it hadn't been before. Haynes's outspoken antislavery beliefs were no longer accepted. The tolerance for Haynes in the pulpit wore thin, and eventually he was dismissed in 1818.

Local tradition relates that when the West Parish congregation realized that Haynes was a man "of color," they dismissed him. Being a mulatto, his lighter complexion didn't seem to matter until the times changed and people became less tolerant and more prejudiced.

Nevertheless, he continued preaching, filling Vermont pulpits in Bennington, Manchester, Middlebury and Pittsfield and Granville, New York.

Haynes was a close acquaintance of abolitionist Vermont governor Richard Skinner (1820–23) and Manchester Underground Railroad agent Joseph Burr. Haynes died at eighty years old in 1836.

RUTLAND

Martin Freeman, a free black, was born in 1826 and raised in Rutland. He attended Middlebury College and graduated as salutatorian in 1849. In 1850, he moved to Pittsburgh, Pennsylvania, and became a professor at the Allegheny Institute, the first black to attain that accomplishment. He excelled in the fields of mathematics and science. He was a black social activist during a very tumultuous era.

In 1856, Freeman was appointed college president of Allegheny Institute, the first African American in the United States to hold this position.

Despite his professional success, Freeman experienced prejudice and racism in Pennsylvania. In Rutland, he had led a sheltered life and was not prepared for the cruelty he faced in the Keystone state.

Colonizationism was gaining ground, and Freeman was a full supporter. He felt that blacks could not achieve respect with the state that the country was in. He knew of the limitations that existed for free blacks. Freeman immigrated to Liberia with his family in 1864. He served as a professor and later as president of Liberia College.

CORINTH AND BROWNINGTON

Alexander Twilight's parents were from New Hampshire. His father was black, and his mother was white. They were the first black family to move to Corinth in 1795, and soon after, Alexander was born. When he was eight, he was indentured to a local farmer but was able to live at home. He worked for the farmer until he was twenty-one years old.

After he left the farm, Twilight enrolled in Orange County Grammar School in Randolph, where he studied for six years, and then he was accepted into Middlebury College. He was the first black man in the United States to earn a college degree, graduating in 1823.

Twilight accepted a teaching job in Vergennes and pastored two churches. He married Mercy, a white woman, in 1826. He took a position at the Orleans County Grammar School in Brownington. Eventually he became the pastor of the Congregational church and served for years there.

Twilight bought large tracts of land in Brownington, as well as a sixty-acre farm close to the school. Twilight tried to get funding for a large dormitory, but the school board refused. So in 1834, Twilight bought land and began construction on a large dormitory himself.

This was no ordinary building that he designed. It took two years to build it from granite boulders, and it was thirty-six feet by sixty-six feet and four stories high. It went in the record books as the first public building made of granite in the state of Vermont. Today, it is preserved and houses the Old Stone House Museum.

He operated the academy for years and received state school funding. Twilight entered politics and was the first black legislator serving in the Vermont legislature in 1836.

Twilight and his wife left Brownington when there were difficulties with school board. But they eventually returned, and the school continued to grow. He was preaching and teaching until his health declined in 1853. Twilight died in 1857.

Twilight left his mark on Vermont history. In 1969, Lyndon State College named a building the Alexander Twilight Theatre. Middlebury College created the Twilight Program, offering fellowships to minority teachers. In 1984, Middlebury College named a restored building for classrooms and seminars after him. His granite Old Stone House stands as a tribute to his ingenuity and dedication.

Part II

THE UNDERGROUND RAILROAD NETWORK

Chapter 5

NETWORKING

Vermonters' Roles

The Underground Railroad was a way to fight slavery directly. Abolitionists chose to take action, knowing that helping one slave to freedom was one step closer to freeing all the slaves. As more slaves escaped and worked their way north, the necessity grew for a network of people to facilitate their escapes. It became apparent that aid couldn't be counted on by chance or luck due to the large number of slaves on the freedom exodus.

The Underground Railroad network is a misunderstood, controversial part of our history. Facts are difficult to separate from stories and information hard to piece together due to its secret nature. Siebert wrote his books in comprehensive, layman terminology so people could understand this complex networking.

Conversations even today about the Underground Railroad are commonly laden with misinformation and misconceptions. Some people, not just children, think it was an actual train that picked up runaways and any house near railroad tracks qualifies as an Underground Railroad safe house. This author has interviewed many Vermont and New Hampshire residents about the subject, and the "train ran right by my uncle's house" too often follows a query. Old houses with unique spaces and secret chambers are typically presumed to be related to the Underground Railroad. That is why it is important to get factual information about the Underground Railroad.

In *Forever Free: The Story of the Emancipation Proclamation*, Dorothy Sterling wrote, "The Underground Railroad wasn't really a railroad, of course. Its tracks were country lanes, its locomotives farm wagons and carriages,

This map of New England depicts major Underground Railroad routes that went through the states including two through Vermont from Massachusetts and New York. *Illustration by Charles E. Metz, architect.*

its conductors ordinary people—Quakers, Yankees, free Negroes, Presbyterians, Jews."

This network of people understood what they had to do to get the job done. Everything was on a word-of-mouth basis. There were no formal meetings, no strategies, no route sheets, no game plans, no membership dues and no handbooks. Once the connections were used, then the next time a fugitive arrived at someone's door, the network would be used again. That pattern turned into a route.

William Breyfogle, author of *Make Free: The Story of the Underground Railroad*, aptly wrote, "Perhaps a majority of agents and conductors never gave a moment's thought to recognition of any kind. The best conductor was the man not known to be a conductor at all, except to those in need of his help. The last thing the Underground wanted was publicity."

Underground Railroad agents did their part with no knowledge of how the slave would fare. Underground Railroad operators were as much in the dark about what was available in Canada as the fugitives were. There was no American-based refugee reception area across the Canadian border.

Working for the slave cause was all about connections and networking. People knew who would be willing to help in a time a need at a moment's notice. The networking was "friend-to-friend." The connections were family, business, former schoolmates, organizations and antislavery societies.

A perfect example of how abolitionists had connections around the state is shown in the officers of the American Antislavery Society from 1834 to 1840. Out of ten officers, six were known Underground Railroad agents in Vermont.

The Reverend Joshua Young, Underground Railroad agent in Burlington, wrote Siebert about his Underground Railroad activity in an April 21, 1893 letter:

> *The UGRR was not…any elaborate system of running off slaves, or indeed of aiding them in their flight, but simply the aiding and passing on from one well known and trusty agent to another, of the fugitives on their way to Canada, and the methods of keeps and concealment employed to secure their safety were as various as the instances of rescue. The chief was to devise ways and means of helping the fugitive in avoiding the central and more public places on his route to Freedom, where the slaveholder might be on especially on the watch for his nimble cattle, that is, to get them round the corner so to speak, which was often done in the early hours of the morning while it was yet dark and in very strange and unsuspected methods of conveyance.*
>
> *We acted as expressmen, watchful and on the alert between the slave states and Canada, and did what was needed, as the case required to deliver our goods in good shape on the other side of that geographical line where their chains fell off as by magic under English Law.*
>
> *As officers of the Road we performed all the functions of station agent, conductor, brakeman and engineer as the case required, and no one called us to an account for exceeding our duty. To give names and dates is impossible as no records were kept; keeping records was dangerous.*

Since there was no map, road signs or highway markers, fugitives had to rely on directions given. In New England, it was more common for fugitives to be taken to the next stop. In Vermont, most of the Underground Railroad agents referred to carrying, conveying or taking fugitives to the next safe house. The distances between towns in rural New England made traveling on foot more time consuming.

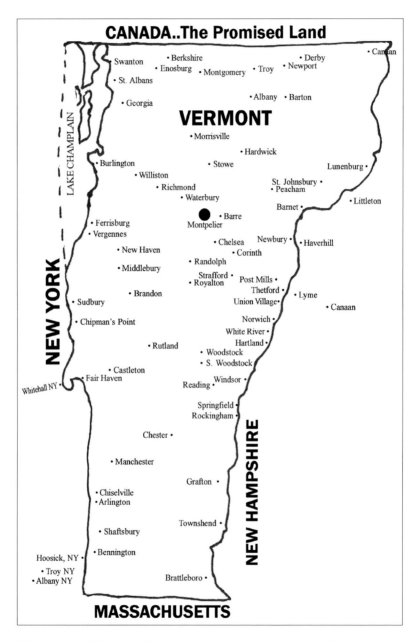

This is a map of Vermont with towns that have connections to the Underground Railroad. There were five main entry points into Vermont for Underground Railroad traffic. From New York state, fugitives came from Albany, Troy and Hoosick agents and also from Whitehall agents. From New Hampshire, traffic came from Canaan, Lyme, Haverhill and Littleton. Also, Vermont received fugitives from Massachusetts agents using the railroad in the late 1840s. *Illustration by Michelle Arnosky Sherburne.*

VERMONT'S ROLE IN THE UNDERGROUND RAILROAD

Vermont's estimated fugitive slave traffic was approximately four thousand from 1820s to 1860s. In connection with the Underground Railroad, I researched seventy-five towns, 135 known Underground Railroad operators and safe houses and thirty-three additional safe houses for which it was hard to determine the occupants at that time.

It has been documented that fugitive slave traffic moved through Vermont towns on a monthly basis. For example, Thetford and Post Mills received fugitives from Canaan and Lyme safehouses once a month. In the 1840 meeting minutes of the Chittenden County Antislavery Society, twelve fugitives had been aided in one year. Burlington had a steady flow of fugitives on a monthly basis.

Aiding fugitive slaves, it could be a one-night experience, or a regular arrangement to accommodate busy traffic coming through the area.

On Vermont's northern border is Canada and all the Underground Railroad maps today show fugitive slave traffic running through its Green Mountains.

ROUTES

Siebert researched and traced patterns of travel through Vermont to create a comprehensive layout of how fugitives moved through the state. These patterns or routes Siebert labeled "trunk lines," using the common nineteenth-century railroad terminology that was commonly used in reference to the Underground Railroad.

Various Underground Railroad documentation cross-references Vermont people and places as being involved with the Underground Railroad. Sometimes it is only a name of a town—i.e., Lunenburg, Vermont—that is referred to, which means digging to uncover the in-depth answers.

In numerous Underground Railroad texts, it is recorded that there were five entry points into Vermont:

- From New York, agents sent fugitives from Whitehall, New York, across the Vermont border to Fair Haven
- From Albany, New York, into Bennington, Vermont
- From Massachusetts to Brattleboro
- From Littleton, New Hampshire to Lunenburg, Vermont
- From either Lyme, New Hampshire, to Post Mills, Vermont, or Haverhill, New Hampshire, to Newbury, Vermont.

Obviously not every fugitive crossed at these points, but patterns show that these were heavily trafficked points of entry.

Essentially, there were two main routes running through the state: a Western route and Eastern Route. Major fugitive traffic junctions in the state were Montpelier and Burlington.

Western Side of Vermont

Fugitive slave traffic moved from New York towns of Albany, Troy and Hoosick and entered Vermont at Bennington. The network ran from Bennington, Manchester, Wallingford, Rutland, Brandon, Middlebury, New Haven, Vergennes, Ferrisburgh and Charlotte to Burlington. Another New York entry point to Vermont was from Whitehall, New York, to Fair Haven, Castleton, Sudbury, Brandon and northward.

Eastern Side of Vermont

Fugitives were sent from Massachusetts safe houses into Vermont at Brattleboro and were taken to Townshend, Grafton, Chester, Cavendish and Ludlow for eventual transport to Woodstock. From Woodstock, the line would run to Norwich, Strafford, Post Mills, Chelsea and Montpelier.

Junction at Vermont's Capitol

A central junction of routes was at Montpelier, and northbound fugitives followed three branches from there. Branch one was from Montpelier to Waterbury, Richmond and Williston and then on to Burlington and north to the Canadian border.

Branch two was from Montpelier to Morrisville, Johnson, Waterville, Cambridge, Enosburg, Montgomery, Berkshire and Franklin before heading on to Canada.

Branch three received fugitives from Montpelier to Hardwick, Barton, Troy and Albany to the Canadian border.

Also on the Eastern Vermont border along the Connecticut River, fugitives traveled from Lyme, New Hampshire, and across the river to Thetford, Post Mills and Chelsea to Montpelier. Also crossing the Connecticut at Haverhill,

New Hampshire, fugitives were passed on to Barnet and Peacham before making their ways north to Canada.

From Littleton, New Hampshire, one of the main points of entry into Vermont, runaways were sent to Lunenburg and hooked into the Eastern Route to Canada.

Out of Burlington to Canada

Once traffic got to Burlington, fugitives were sent up through the Lake Champlain Islands directly into Canada at Rouses Point. Fugitives also traveled from Burlington to Georgia, north to St. Albans and then either by boat or railroad to Canada. Branch three from Burlington was to Swanton and then to Franklin before making it to Canada.

AGENTS

Peeling back the layers of Vermont's past, we discover the major contribution that Vermonters made in the Underground Railroad network. The list must begin with the renowned Robinson family in Ferrisburgh.

Vermont's well-known Underground Railroad safe house was operated by Rowland Thomas and Rachel Gilpin Robinson. Five generations of Robinsons lived on this property known as Rokeby, which today is the Rokeby Museum on Route 7 in Ferrisburgh. The museum's collection is a vast array of Americana and Vermont history from the late eighteenth

Rowland Thomas and Rachel Gilpin Robinson were famous Underground Railroad agents in Ferrisburgh, Vermont. This daguerreotype of the Robinsons is in the Rokeby Museum collection. *Courtesy of Rokeby Museum.*

century to the twentieth century. The Robinson families saved everything including letters, butter molds, farm equipment, paintings, furniture, books, photographs, pottery and cookware.

The Three Rs: Rokeby, Rowland and Rachel

Thomas and Jemima Robinson were Rhode Island natives who were Quakers and abolitionists. They moved to Vermont in 1791 and had only two children: Rowland T. and Abigail Robinson Hoag. Thomas's farm was known as Rokeby and was a thriving farm with the first and largest sheep herd in the state, apple and pear orchards and a sawmill and a gristmill that provided employment in the small rural community.

Education was important to the Robinsons, and Rowland T. was sent to Nine Partners, a Quaker boarding school founded by an ardent abolitionist Elias Hicks in Washington, New York. Students were taught that eliminating the slavery institution was the main purpose of the abolitionist cause. Alumnus of Nine Partners were famous abolitionists and Underground Railroad agents like Daniel Anthony (Susan B. Anthony's father) and Lucretia and James Mott.

While at Nine Partners, Rowland met his soul mate in Rachel Gilpin, and they were married in 1820. The newlyweds returned to Rokeby, where Rowland took over the reins and worked with Thomas. Rowland and Rachel's children were Thomas, born in 1823; George, in 1825; Ann, in 1827; and Rowland Evan, in 1833. Rokeby eventually had a large nuclear family with grandparents, parents, children and grandchildren living under the same roof.

Rowland T. was prosperous and increased Rokeby's holdings to one thousand acres and two thousand head of Merino sheep. He hired farm managers, and many of his abolitionist friends would send fugitive slaves to Rokeby for work opportunities. Some would stay, but others were Canada-bound.

Rokeby consisted of a farmhouse, tourist cabin, kitchen and woodshed building, smokehouse, henhouse, creamery, granary, dairy barn, sheep barn, field barn, schoolhouse and other outbuildings.

The Robinsons believed that educating blacks would lead to better lives, and in that vein, Rowland helped establish the New York Association of Friends for the Relief of Those Held in Slavery and also the Improvement of the Free People of Color in 1839. The outreach of these two organizations was supporting schools in New York City.

The two-story schoolhouse was open from 1839 to 1846 and called the "Brick Academy." Teachers were hired and, besides the Robinsons' own children, the other attendees were area children, fugitive slave children and adults. Fugitive slaves who stayed extended periods were taught to read and write.

Rowland and Rachel were both active abolitionists. They were staunch Garrisonians who believed that there was no biblical justification for slavery and that all men were created by God equally. Their biggest contribution to the antislavery cause was welcoming fugitive slaves into their home and helping them start new lives or helping them continue their journeys to Canada and freedom.

Rowland was one of the founding members of the Vermont Antislavery Society, along with his father, Thomas, and served as its executive chairman in 1834. Closer to home, he helped found the Ferrisburgh Antislavery Society. He joined the American Antislavery Society and traveled extensively around New England to promote the abolitionist cause. He funded distribution of antislavery literature.

Rowland corresponded with big players of the national antislavery cause, such as William Lloyd Garrison, Oliver Johnson, Orson Murray, Charles C. Bruleigh, Lucretia Mott and Isaac Hopper. The Robinsons were well-known abolitionists throughout the country, highly respected and revered.

At the second-annual meeting of the Ferrisburgh Antislavery Society in 1836, Rowland promoted abstaining from using slave-labor products that "are believed to come to us from a polluted channel." In their own home, Rowland and Rachel boycotted slave-labor products, like sugar, rice, coffee, cotton, molasses, tobacco, fabric and flour. They wrote letter campaigns, and Rachel lectured on the subject. Garrison commended her efforts in an 1835 letter, stating that "her practice corresponds admirably with her doctrine."

In 1843, the New England Anti-Slavery Society held a series of one hundred conventions in New Hampshire, Vermont, New York, Ohio, Indiana and Pennsylvania. Rowland organized and hosted the "Great Convention" in North Ferrisburgh in July 1843. Famous lecturers included Frederick Douglass, George Bradburn, James Monroe, William A. White, Charles L. Remond, Sydney Howard Gay and John A. Collins.

Rokeby: An Underground Railroad Station

From 1830 to the late 1840s, Rokeby was a very busy Underground Railroad station and the Rokeby Museum collection has correspondence from

This is the main house at Rokeby from the southwest corner of the property. *Courtesy of Rokeby Museum.*

this timeframe about fugitives being sent there. The letters refer to slaves en route to Rokeby or of their progress North. It is valuable evidence of Underground Railroad activity.

Rowland and Rachel had many ties to the New York Quakers who sent fugitives to them. There was a chain of Quaker communities from New York City to Vermont. Fergus Bordewich wrote in a July 2005 article, "Quakers could travel from New York to Burlington without ever sleeping beneath a non-Quaker's roof. So could fugitives."

Rowland was the principal player in charge of receiving, retrieving, planning and transporting them onward. Other adults in the household helped take care of fugitives like his parents, Rachel and friend Anne King.

Unlike some situations of Underground Railroad assistance, at Rokeby, fugitive slaves were not always hidden and transferred at night. The Robinsons had fugitives working on the farm, out in the fields and in the house. Ferrisburgh is a remote area in rural Vermont, so having blacks working in the fields in Ferrisburgh would not be that obvious since it was not in the middle of town.

New England abolitionists knew that Rokeby was a large farm that could always use the extra farm help and was a secure place. Correspondence often mentioned slaves' skills and sounded more like work referrals. Other letters refered to Rokeby as being a better place than Canada for the fugitives.

Oliver Johnson, fellow Vermonter and famous abolitionist in Pennsylvania, wrote Robinson in January 1837 about a fugitive slave, Simon. "He is 28 years old and appeared to me to be an honest, likely man…I was so well pleased with his appearance…that I could not help thinking he would be a good man for you to hire. Mr. Griffith says that he is very trustworthy, of a kind disposition, and knows how to do almost all kinds of farm work. He is used to teaming, and is very good to manage horses. He says that he could beat any man in the neighborhood where he lived at mowing, cradling or pitching."

It was a common abolitionist belief that fugitives were safer under the supervision and protection of someone like Robinson rather than sending them to Canada. Rokeby was a guaranteed place for work, education and guidance. Up until the 1850 Fugitive Slave Law, abolitionists wanted fugitive slaves to stay in the United States.

It is important to note that not every fugitive was safe on his way to Rokeby. It was on a case-by-case basis. The Robinsons' granddaughter Mary Robinson Perkins related a story at a 1921 women's club meeting that she had heard from her father about "a Southerner [who] came to Vergennes, four miles away, looking for a slave who had just been taken north from our place."

Rowland also had fellow Underground Railroad agent Samuel Barker in neighboring Vergennes act as a lookout for any slave hunters in the area. It was Barker's responsibility to alert Burlington agents of any suspicious characters.

When son Rowland E. Robinson responded to Wilbur Siebert's first questionnaire in 1896, he wrote that when he was about ten years old, he recalled "seeing four fugitives at a time in my father's house and quite often one or two harboring there." The memory was vivid due to the fact that one of the fugitives "carried the first pistols I ever saw and other [illegible] the first bowie knife."

All in the Family

The Robinson Underground Railroad activity is a great example of networking using family connections. From Ferrisburgh to East Montpelier, Rowland knew he had relatives who worked for the cause and would help fugitives.

Underground Railroad agent Nathan Dodge lived on Sibley Road in East Montpelier and was related to Rowland Robinson. Stories have been passed down of Dodge hiding numerous fugitive slaves, and it is said that his neighbor Addison Peck helped him occasionally. In the "Peck Family

Papers," Peck wrote of finding a fugitive hidden in his hayloft. Dodge had left the slave there, and Peck's wife fed him breakfast before Peck drove him ten miles to another safe house.

Rowland T.'s sister Abigail and her husband, Nathan Hoag, of Charlotte, operated a nearby Underground Railroad safe house in a secluded location, and sometimes fugitives stayed for months, helping on the farm and in the house.

Deit C. Dail, of East Montpelier and a friend of Rowland's, delivered fugitives to his nephew Stephen Foster Stevens in East Montpelier. Stevens was a cabinetmaker, farmer and a Quaker minister. He invented the Stevens platform scale. In 1855, he served as a representative to the Vermont legislature. Fugitives stayed for weeks at a time or for the summer. Stevens was in the loop from 1830 to 1850 receiving fugitives.

A mile north of Ferrisburgh and Rokeby was the home of Joseph Rogers, who was a close friend of the Robinsons. Rogers was referred to in an 1878 letter from William Lloyd Garrison to Rowland T., and son Rowland E. also wrote Siebert about Joseph Rogers's assistance. In a diary entry from the mid-1840s, Joseph's sister Morah wrote about Robinson delivering a fugitive slave to their house. Then Joseph took him to Charlotte to board a boat on Lake Champlain.

From the Source: Letters

The letters in the Rokeby Museum letter collection provide us with a glimpse of the Underground Railroad activity and fugitive slaves sent to the Robinsons. The letters date from 1837, 1842, 1844 and 1851 and refer to specific cases of fugitives' experiences or fugitives being sent to Rokeby.

Rachel wrote in a January 9, 1844 letter to family friend Anne King in New York about two fugitive slaves who were anxious to get to Canada, though they had to leave their wives behind. Rachel wrote that the two men "were afraid to remain anywhere within our glorious republic lest the chain of servitude should again bind soul and limb…they tarried with [us] only one night & were very anxious to journey on to Victoria's domain…They left wives behind and deeply did they appear to feel the separation."

Thomas received a letter in May 1851 from James Temple, a fugitive slave he had helped back in 1846. Temple was living in Montreal, Quebec. Thomas had given him a pair of his late wife's glasses, and Temple wrote to thank him. Temple wrote, "I am at work at my trade getting a living looking through the glasses you gave me for which I never shall forget to be thankful. I think that I shall soon be able to send for my family if I conclude to stay here…I am happy to testify the pleasure I feel in ever becoming acquainted with you and of partaking of your benefits which was so liberally and willingly [tendered?] to me by your beautiful hands."

In 1837, Rowland T. wrote letters to slave owner Ephram Elliott of North Carolina trying to negotiate a slave's freedom papers. The owner wouldn't lower his price, but Rowland tried. Unfortunately, the slave could not buy his freedom.

Garrison held the Robinsons in high regard as active abolitionists. In an 1878 letter to Rowland T., Garrison wrote, "I always placed you high on my list of friends and co-laborers the most esteemed and the truest; and it affords me the greatest satisfaction to know that you have been preserved to hear the ringing of the jubilee bell, and to witness all those marvelous changes which have taken place in our land within less than a score of years."

The Slave Room at Rokeby

Rokeby has a room was in the "east chamber" that for generations was called "the slave room." The slave room could have been the quarters used for fugitive slaves or for the blacks who stayed and lived at Rokeby. In 1859 correspondence between Rowland's sons George and Rowland E., they refer to black servants who lived and worked in the house when they were adults.

Mary Robinson Perkins, the daughter of Rowland Evans Robinson and granddaughter of Rowland and Rachel, wrote an introduction in the book *Out of Bondage* about the slave room. This book was published after her father's death in 1900. Perkins wrote, "The Robinson home was a 'station,' and there is a room in it—the 'east chamber'—which was often called the 'slave room.' It is not a hidden room, but the doorway is inconspicuous and at the far end of another bedroom. There the runaway slaves found a comfortable harbor. My father and his sister and brothers were never allowed to ask any questions about meals that were taken by Aunt Anne King up the back-stairs to this room, but they understood from the act that a dusky fugitive was stopping there for a little while. The travellers were always taken by team at night to the next 'station' nearer Canada."

End of Their Underground Railroad Business

In abolitionist circles, tension increased because some, like Rowland, disagreed with gradual emancipation and wanted immediate, direct action. By 1843, Rowland and his cohorts resigned from the Vermont Antislavery Society, and he lost his footing in the American Antislavery Society as well because those with his views were considered radical.

Around 1850, Rokeby's traffic slowed drastically. Rowland E. wrote Siebert that he didn't remember "seeing a [illegible] fugitive here after 1850, though now and then an imposter called on us." This change was due to what was going on at Rokeby and not nationally.

At this time, the Robinsons lost their Quaker and abolitionist connections, plus Rokeby was struggling because sheep production had dropped off drastically and wool prices dropped. The farm was in financial trouble, and the Robinsons focused on that.

Their Quaker connections failed because the Robinsons' strong Hicksite beliefs were unpopular, and Roland and Rachel left the Society of Friends in 1850. That meant they lost Underground Railroad ties with the New York Quakers.

Around this time, the Robinsons turned to spiritualism, as did many in the 1850s, holding séances in their home. Spiritualism did not bode well with the Quakers they knew, and the family was ostracized even more.

Rachel died in 1862, unable to see the fruits of their abolitionist labors. Rowland T. lived to see the Emancipation Proclamation and slavery abolished in the United States.

Rowland T. continued his efforts for education for Negroes, making donations to Negro colleges and offering employment and shelter for blacks. He fought the fight into his eighties. He was a temperance activist, who fought for women's rights and sought relief for the poor and homeless. In all of Rowland's efforts, he gave himself wholeheartedly before he died in 1879 at the age of eighty-three.

He and Rachel left a visible mark in the history of abolition on the local, state and national levels. They spent their entire lives fighting slavery without wavering. More importantly, Rowland and Rachel helped hundreds of fugitive slaves to freedom. Rokeby was a successful station and is a tribute to this couple and their Underground Railroad efforts, as well as an historic treasure of Vermont life through the ages.

SPRINGFIELD

Noah Safford witnessed slavery firsthand when he traveled to Southern states marketing his hay and straw cutter machine and dedicated his life to helping slaves through Vermont to freedom.

Noah Safford was the son of a Revolutionary War veteran and was raised in Rockingham. In the early 1820s, Safford invented a straw cutter that became a popular piece of farm equipment. The March 29, 1823 issue of *The American Farmer* of Boston, Massachusetts, promoted his equipment:

Safford's Straw Cutter.— We have seen a Machine in operation for cutting straw, &c. invented by Mr. Noah Safford, of Springfield, Vermont, which we believe to combine more advantages than any other ever put in use, taking into consideration its cheapness, simplicity, &c. We are well assure that it will cut, with the moderate labor of one man, a bushel of straw in a minute, or sixty bushels in an hour. The notice of the improvement which is given in Mr. S.'s advertisement, together with the testimonial in its favor, bearing the signatures of persons who are good judges of the merits of machinery of this sort, supersede the necessity of any other remarks from us.

Noah Safford, 1790–1863, is buried in the Summer Street Cemetery in Springfield, Vermont. Safford and his wife, Nancy, were Underground Railroad agents in Springfield. *Courtesy of* History of the Town of Springfield.

By 1829, Safford marketed his product from Boston to Richmond, Virginia, spending winters down South. In his travels, he saw slave auctions in progress and witnessed children taken from mothers' arms as the auctioneer finalized the deal. He visited plantations and saw the horrible treatment of slaves.

SAFFORD'S STRAW CUTTER.

THE utility of cutting Hay, Straw, and other sub-
stances for feeding cattle, is now so universally
acknowledged that any remarks on the subject must
be deemed superfluous. The following Certificate will
therefore be conclusive of the merits of the above mentioned Machine.

Boston, March 22, 1823.

We, the subscribers, have in operations a Straw
Cutting Machine invented and exhibited in this city by
Noah Safford, and we do not hesitate to say that in our
opinion it exceeds any other we have ever seen, for
cheapness, simplicity, despatch and durability.

**STEPHEN HARTWELL, SPURR & HOLMES,
HEZEKIAH EARL, ANDREW SLATER.**

The above mentioned Machines may be had of
J. R. NEWELL, at the Agricultural Establishment,
No. 20, Merchant's Row, Boston, Price $15.

This is a rendition of an advertisement for Noah Safford's straw cutter that was reviewed in the March 29, 1823 *American Farmer Magazine. Courtesy of Michelle Arnosky Sherburne.*

These images burned into Noah's brain, heart and soul. In the *Folklore of Springfield Vermont,* author Eva M. Baker wrote that Safford "saw enough of slavery to make him vow eternal vengeance upon it."

Back in Vermont, Noah and his wife, Nancy, decided to fight the slavery institution any way they could. They became part of the Underground Railroad network and opened their home for passing fugitive slaves. Siebert referred to them as a team, saying that Nancy was "just the sort of person to share in his Underground labors."

Like the Robinson family of Ferrisburgh, the Saffords boycotted Southern products. They also boycotted the American Board, which was a national organization orchestrating American missions because it received funding from slave owners. In Springfield, Noah demanded that speakers from the abolitionist lecture circuit be allowed to speak in lecture halls or in church. People knew where he stood on issues, especially about slavery.

Their daughter, Rebecca Safford Holmes, related her parents' Underground Railroad activities to Mary Baker for the *History of Springfield* published in 1894. The Safford home was known as "one of the good places to visit, where a generous hospitality was dispensed."

Fugitive slave traffic came from New York to Manchester and traveled through the mountains east to Springfield. Holmes remembered wagons arriving at night with fugitives and Noah hiding them in the barn. Noah took food out to the barn in the morning for the visitors.

Depending on the situation, fugitives would stay overnight and the next evening be taken to Perkinsville or North Springfield. Sometimes they would have to stay for days, hidden in the barn or in the attic until it was safe. Noah transported them by wagon to safe houses in Perkinsville or North Springfield.

Locally, Noah was a successful businessman with a foundry business, woodshop, factory and mill. But socially, the Saffords were kept at a distance. Noah and Nancy paid a price for standing up for their abolitionist beliefs: they were ostracized by the community.

BENNINGTON

Bennington is close to New York's Hudson River Valley, which was a main eastern route for runaway slaves. In this town, the heavy runaway traffic was handled by the father and son team of Charles and Henry Hicks. Using his connections as a stagecoach driver, Charles received many fugitives. Much of the Hickses' involvement in the Underground Railroad is documented in letters.

The Hickses' letters are wonderful examples showing the fluctuating atmosphere during the Antebellum period, spelling out the way things changed depending on the politics of the country with regard to the slavery issue. These letters are valuable not only for their proof of documentation but also because of the information regarding the workings of the Underground Railroad in Vermont.

One of the Hickses' New York connections was the Reverend Abel Brown of Sand Lake, New York, who was recorded as aiding one thousand slaves during his career. Information gathered through the Hicks-Brown correspondence shows fugitive traffic moved from northern New York to Bennington regularly.

An 1843 letter documented son Henry's role, which was to transport a fugitive family from Bennington to the Simon Bottum farm in Shaftsbury, a frequent destination for runaway slaves.

Parts of a November 24, 1840 letter from Fayette Shipherd, an Underground
Railroad agent in Hoosick, New York, to Bennington's agent Charles Hicks: "As
the canal has closed I shall send my Southern friends along your road & patronize
your house. We had a fine run of business during the season. C.G. We had 22 in
two weeks 13 in the city at one time…A Baltimore officer—a man hunter was seen
in our city making his observations but left without giving us any trouble. Several
slaves were in our city from Baltimore at the time." *Courtesy of Vermont Historical Society
collection. Hicks letter from Fayette Shipherd.*

In the Underground Railroad networks, the usage of introduction letters
was common. The recipient of the letter knew that the letter bearer was a
safe person who needed help, with recommendations from the last person
who helped them. The well-known Hicks letter shows that it was carried by

a runaway and originated from the Reverend Abel Brown to introduce the bearer to Hicks: "Dear Sir, Please receive the Bearer as a friend who needs your aid and direct him on his way if you cannot give him work he comes to us well recommended was a slave a few weeks since." The letter was signed as "cor Secy of Eastern N.Y. Aslavery Socy."

An 1840 letter written by the Reverend Fayette Shipherd, Underground Railroad agent in Hoosick, New York, to Hicks conveys that Shipherd was cautious about his identity being discovered. "I shall hereafter merely give you address on a card, as [more converts?] to carry. My hand you will know. Nov. 24, 1840."

Every situation was different. Danger was more of an issue at some times versus others. Fugitives arrived at different times, and each case had to be handled accordingly. In some letters, there were warnings of slave catchers in the Albany, New York area. Sometimes Bennington and surrounding areas were not safe places for fugitives.

The 1842 letter is detailed and openly identifies who the operators were. On the contrary, two letters dated 1840 and 1843 are more discreet and show that there must have been need for cautiousness and secrecy because obvious danger existed.

The importance of secrecy is evidenced in an 1843 letter written by daughter Eliza Hicks. The letter tells of a fugitive family sheltered at the Hickses' home, and Eliza wrote about the people and places involved. At the end of the letter are direct instructions to destroy after reading for safety's sake: "Please burn this as soon as you read it…let no one see it."

WOODSTOCK

In Woodstock and Vermont, the Honorable Titus Hutchinson was a well-known public figure, a man who was highly respected. His accomplishments were numerous, but one area of his devotion never surfaced in the accolades: his Underground Railroad efforts. Hutchinson aided fugitive slaves in secret through Woodstock. Many fugitives passed north to Hutchinson from Colonel Thomas Powers in South Woodstock or from Perkinsville.

Fugitives were hidden in the Hutchinson house located on the corner of Elm Street and Central Street in the heart of Woodstock village at the beginning of the Green.

Left: This is a daguerreotype of Titus Hutchinson, 1771–1857, a prominent Woodstock, Vermont citizen who secretly aided fugitive slaves at his house in the center of Woodstock. *Courtesy of the Woodstock Historical Society Inc. collection. Photo of daguerreotype by Michelle Arnosky Sherburne.*

Below: This is an 1860 photo of the Titus Hutchinson house, pictured on the left next to the tree, which was and still is one of Woodstock's most prominent houses "on the Green." His house was at the corner of Elm and Central Streets with the Barkers Hotel across the street. *Photograph courtesy of the Woodstock Historical Society.*

In the 1986 "Underground Railroad in Vermont and New Hampshire" pamphlet, it stated that an underground tunnel running from the Hutchinson home to the Kedron River, which weaves its way beside Woodstock, had been discovered during bridge construction. The tunnel, approximately four-tenths of a mile long, was then filled in.

Hutchinson sent fugitives to Strafford or Royalton safe houses. Though Woodstock had a small black population, Hutchinson kept his work secret from his neighbors and friends.

People knew Hutchinson was an abolitionist, a tireless writer of letters to the newspapers airing his views about slavery and the illegality of the Fugitive Slave Act of 1850.

The *History of Woodstock, Vt.* noted that Hutchinson was "a person of great distinction and carried in his single hand the official force of several majors and colonels," which steered him in politics, running for Congress from 1810 to 1825. Hutchinson was nominated by President James Madison to serve as U.S. attorney representing Vermont for a decade. In 1826, he continued to escalate and was nominated as State Supreme Court judge for four years. He was then elected chief judge, an office he held for three years.

He married late in life, at age twenty-nine, to Clarissa Sage, and they had five sons and one daughter. Interestingly, one son, Oramel, followed his father's lead as an Underground Railroad operator in Chester and helped fugitive slaves there.

Hutchinson was very active in the community, serving as postmaster, town representative for ten years and as part of Woodstock's branch of Vermont State Bank. He was active in the abolitionist movement in his public life, profession and political career, and he did not falter in his work for the fugitive slaves.

After 1833, he retired and farmed for twenty years. Titus died in 1857.

Taking into consideration his stature, public life, profession and political career, it is particularly admirable that he was also so faithful to the Underground Railroad cause.

STRAFFORD AND NORWICH

Sylvester Morris was a driving force where he lived and worked. He was known as a compassionate man, a hard worker and a successful businessman. Kate Morris Cone wrote a biography about her grandfather, *A Sketch of the Life of Sylvester Morris*, in 1887, in which she said:

> But his life-work, and the thing for which he is to be especially remembered, was his position regarding the two great social questions of his day. He was the local apostle of anti-slavery and temperance in the towns in which

Sylvester Morris, an Underground Railroad agent in Strafford and Norwich, Vermont, had successful businesses and helped many slaves. *Courtesy of "A Sketch of Sylvester Morris" by Kate Eugenia (Morris) Cone, 1887, Google documents.*

he lived, and threw himself into the promotion of each cause with all the energy of his strong nature.

As an abolitionist he employed the methods for arousing public opinion which were common to the cause…He became a sort of public conscience, a "character," in the streets and public places in Norwich, and no occasion was too common or adversary too high or low for his attacks…It was his custom, also, to hold public discussions upon anti-slavery in the church vestry at Norwich, with any one who would engage with him.

As regards that famous institution, by which many a fugitive slave was handed on from one friendly house to another, public sentiment in Vermont was too undecided, and the Canada line too near, to make the harboring of slaves in Norwich particularly dangerous. Danger or not, a room was devoted to such guests in the Morris house, and there, sometimes, for several days, the poor creatures were sheltered, the women often gladly taking part in the work of the household.

The Morrises were selfless people, always willing to help someone in need. George S. Morris, Sylvester's son, shared with college friend John L. Brewster about his father's Norwich Underground Railroad safe house. George remembered as a boy going downstairs to breakfast, where a whole table of "colored people would be eating their breakfast—No member of the family ever asked a question about them as to when they came or were to go or when." Brewster and George graduated in 1861, and years later, after George had died, Brewster wrote Siebert in 1896.

Up until 1826, the Strafford Turnpike was a heavily traveled route that ran from Boston to Burlington, continuing on to Montreal, Quebec. This made Strafford a busy junction for another form of traffic: two Underground Railroad routes. From the south, fugitive slaves came from Woodstock, and from the east, connections stemmed from the Lyme, New Hampshire route. Since the established turnpike continued to Chelsea, Morris's guests traveled that way often.

Cone wrote about her grandfather's fervor about the slavery issue: "Deacon Morris was our rough, hard-handed Abolitionist tanner. He was the local apostle of antislavery and temperance in the towns in which he lived...he took extreme and absolute ground."

Morris was a native of Stafford, Connecticut. He married Susannah of Randolph, Vermont, in 1822, and their first years together in that state were in Barnard. He was a farmer but then got into the tanning business. They moved to Strafford in Vermont in 1827. They had ten children, and one of their sons, George, became a noted educator, philosophical writer and lecturer at University of Michigan and Johns Hopkins University.

Morris bought a tannery in South Strafford but may have lived in the village of South Strafford. In the 1830 census, he is listed among village households. The Morrises joined the Strafford Congregational Church in 1828, and four years later, Sylvester became a deacon of that church. The title of "deacon" became part of his name for the rest of his life, as he was referred to as "Deacon Morris." Morris was an officer in the newly organized First Congregational Society of Strafford, and a new church was built in 1832.

The Morrises helped fugitives while living in Strafford and Norwich. Siebert recorded that while in Strafford, Morris transported fugitives to Moses Smith's in Lyme, New Hampshire, or to Mr. Lord's in Union Village.

Norwich Years

After ten years in Strafford, the Morrises moved south to Norwich. Wherever their home was, Deacon Morris and Susanna continued their Underground Railroad efforts and a room was set aside for fugitive slave guests.

Ada L. Brewster wrote in a May 20, 1895 letter to Siebert: "At Norwich Vermont—just across the river from Hanover, lived a Mr. Morris, a worthy deacon in the Congregational Church, who was well known to have aided and helped to Canada any slaves who required his assistance."

Morris was involved in different manufacturing ventures in Norwich. He owned a fulling and cloth-dressing mill, a tannery and a shoe and leather

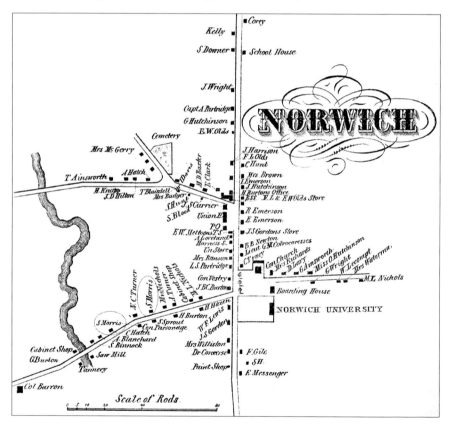

This 1856 print of Norwich is from the *Map of Windsor County, VT 1856* by Hosea Doton. On the left side of the street, "S Morris" has two buildings listed, one of which was the first house that the Morris family lived in when they moved to Norwich. The map also shows the tannery and sawmill on the river that Morris operated. In later years, the Morrises moved onto the main street in what was known as the 1820 house. *Courtesy of Dave Allen at www.old-maps.com, P.O. Box 54, West Chesterfield, New Hampshire, 03466.*

store in Hanover, New Hampshire. In 1853, he built a plaster mill, which he sold to sons Edward and Ephraim in 1857. They turned it into a chair manufacturing plant.

The Morrises joined the Norwich Congregational Church, and Sylvester served as deacon for thirty-seven years. They welcomed ministers, missionaries and abolitionists in their home.

In 1843, the Norwich Female Abolition Society was established by seventeen women in the Norwich Congregational Church, including Susannah and daughter Huldah. In the Norwich Female Abolition Society minutes is an interesting perspective of women's connections to the oppressed slaves: "And, more especially, in relation to the suffering of our own sex who are deprived of personal liberty, would we not forget this Apostle's injunction, 'Remember those in bonds, so bound with them.'"

Vermont had five female antislavery societies on record in Bellingham, Weybridge, Cornwall, Norwich and Randolph. Since women were not allowed to join most antislavery societies, they decided to form their own.

The sewing circles became the popular activity of women's church groups and female antislavery societies that popped up during the 1830s. Sewing circles were outlets to sew quilts, shirts, dresses and pants to donate to the Underground Railroad cause.

The Norwich women worked diligently for the cause of the slaves. During sewing circle meetings, the women were updated on the latest news from abolitionist newspapers and had special events with guest speakers.

They received thank-you letters, such as one from Reverend Hiram Wilson in Rochester, New York, dated June 13, 1844, that stated: "Your very acceptable box of clothing from Norwich, Vt. has been received. Also your very welcome and cheering communication contained in the box and dated Oct. 6, 1843. Permit me to express to you in behalf of my fellow labourers and in behalf of the afflicted and benighted poor in Canada escaped from American Slavery our sincere thanks for the interest manifested by yourself and the Society with which you are connected, in our holy cause."

Another shipment went to Henry Highland Garnet in Troy, New York, a former Noyes Academy student, who wrote them saying the items would be used "for the benefit of the fugitives that should call on him for help." In a letter dated December 18, 1844, that was read at one of their meetings, he wrote about a fugitive slave he had recently helped.

The Morrises made their mark in the annals in Underground Railroad history. Cone wrote, "At last, after 40 years of working and waiting, [Morris] saw that stupendous change in public opinion."

At age sixty, Sylvester traveled from Norwich to Hartford over the rough roads to tend to his businesses. Sadly, he outlived Susannah by nineteen years, eventually dying in 1886.

THETFORD CENTER

Across the Connecticut River in Lyme, New Hampshire, Underground Railroad agents were kept busy with a monthly flow of fugitives brought from Canaan, New Hampshire. A network within Lyme was set up by several residents to accommodate the influx. Lyme agents transported fugitives across the Vermont border to the Thetford and Post Mills agents. A glimpse of how the night deliveries of the Lyme agents worked exists in eyewitness accounts from two men who grew up in these towns.

The late Thetford historian Mary Slade was compiling information for a town history and was told the following story by a Midwest man who had grown up in Lyme. In the evening, his father took him to deliver a load of hay to Post Mills. When they arrived at Deacon Hinckley's house, he was sent into the house and told not to say anything about the trip. As soon as the hay was unloaded, his father came for him and they returned home. He was not allowed to talk about that night delivery.

Martha Howard of the Thetford Historical Society said that Thetford Hill resident Dr. Ezra Worcester helped fugitives. He had a medical wagon with black curtains for privacy that he used for house calls and to transport patients. It wouldn't be suspicious for Dr. Worcester to be out running the roads at all hours of the night.

Slade wrote Siebert about the doctor's wagon and said that she had interviewed Worcester's grandson. She learned that the doctor sometimes transported fugitive slaves under the pretense of night medical trips. He would make a run to Lyme when fugitives were expected and pick them up and transfer them to Thomas Sanborn's house in Thetford Center.

Dr. Ezra Carter Worcester was born in 1816 in Peacham and married Ellen Hunt from Charlestown, New Hampshire, in 1836. Worcester received a medical degree from Dartmouth College in 1838 and practiced medicine in St. Johnsbury, Chelsea and Thetford. The Worcester family moved to Thetford Hill in 1846, where their residence had a medical dispensary. In addition to his medical practice and involvement with Thetford Academy in 1850, Worcester also established one of the earliest commercial nurseries in the state. Worcester died in 1887.

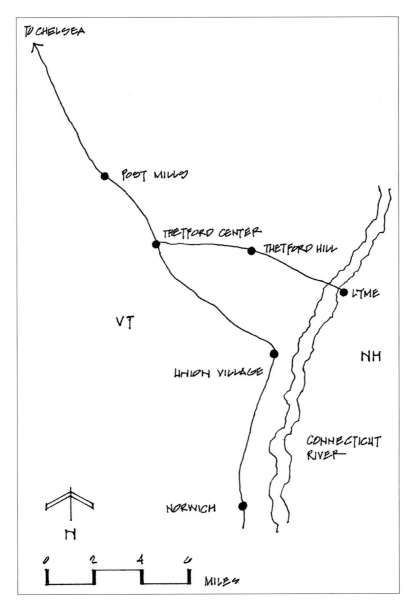

This is a rendition of a map drawn by Mary Slade of Thetford and sent to
Wilbur Siebert for his Underground Railroad research. Underground Railroad
agents in Norwich and Union Village took fugitives to Post Mills. But the main
source was from Lyme, New Hampshire. The distance from Lyme, crossing the
Connecticut River, is four miles to Thetford Center, where the Sanborn house
is located. From Thetford Center, it is three miles to Lyman Hinckley's house.
Then it is approximately fifteen miles from Hinckley's to Chelsea, the next stop.
Illustration by Charles E. Metz, architect.

Thomas Sanborn

The Thomas Sanborn House, the present-day E.C. Brown Greenhouses property on Route 113 in Thetford Center, was known as a station on the Underground Railroad. Transported from Lyme into Vermont, the fugitives were taken to Sanborn's house in Thetford Center. Through a hidden door in the summer kitchen in the back of the house, slaves were hidden in a root cellar. An opening in the root cellar led to an underground tunnel that ran the distance of the summer kitchen to the barn on the back of the property, where they could board a wagon, unseen.

Locals remember the underground tunnel, which kids used to play in up until the 1940s when it was blocked for safety reasons. The summer kitchen was torn down years later.

Slade wrote Siebert in 1943, saying she was told by Sanborn's grandson that his father "used to tell him of waking in the night and seeing a negro go thro the room."

For years, the Sanborn house was known locally as an Underground Railroad stop. Postcards refer to that distinction, and information about an underground tunnel from a summer kitchen to the barn has been shared. *Courtesy of Thetford Historical Society.*

Sanborn was born in Enfield, New Hampshire, in 1805 and was active in Grafton, New Hampshire, as a justice of the peace and grand juror and was prominent in town. He married Mary in 1830 and lived in Springfield, New Hampshire. Their first son was born in 1834 in Springfield.

Six years and six children later, the Sanborns moved to Thetford in 1840. The Sanborns lived with Hezekiah Porter in his house on Thetford Hill while building their home. Incidentally, the Hezekiah Porter House is another known Underground Railroad station. Sanborn lived the rest of his life in town, working as a stone and brick mason until he died in 1880.

Another interesting fact was that Sanborn's oldest son, Alonson, was a lieutenant in the Vermont Company B, First U.S. Colored

Thomas Sanborn of Thetford Center received fugitive slaves from Lyme and took them to the next safe house in Post Mills. *Courtesy of Thetford Historical Society.*

Volunteers in the Civil War. In 1862, Alonson was a recruiter in New York City for a regiment of black soldiers. It was a week after the Battle of Gettysburg and the fall of Vicksburg when Lieutenant Sanborn led his troops to the Custom House for review. On the way to Custom House, someone insulted his black troops. Sanborn reprimanded the man, and after he turned, the reprimanded soldier shot him in the back. He died in July 1863, at age twenty-nine, in Norfolk, Virginia. The man was arrested and tried. President Abraham Lincoln was instrumental in selecting the witnesses. The shooter was found guilty and hanged.

Post Mills

The Thetford Historical Society 2012 Vermont History Expo display featured information about Post Mills resident Lyman Hinckley's involvement in the

Underground Railroad. "From these locations, slaves would travel about 10 miles west to Post Mills where directly across from the Chubb/Malmquist site, Lyman Hinckley would conceal slaves in a closet under a staircase in his home."

In Post Mills, a village in the town of Thetford, one name that frequently surfaces in letters, histories and accounts with regard to the Underground Railroad is Deacon Lyman Hinckley. Post Mills received traffic from the Norwich to Strafford to Union Village route or the Canaan to Lyme, New Hampshire route. These routes were used during the busy years of the Underground Railroad.

It is four miles from Lyme, New Hampshire, to Thetford Center where the Sanborn house is located. From Thetford Center, it is three miles to Lyman Hinckley's house. Then it is approximately fifteen miles from Hinckley's to Chelsea, the next stop.

Hinckley's home was a large brick, three-story house across from the Hinckle Linseed Oil Mill, which was later the Chubb fishing rod factory. Once delivered to Hinckley, he hid fugitives in the barn and then transported them north to Wilder Dearborn's farm in Chelsea.

Deacon Lyman Hinckley was an Underground Railroad agent in Post Mills and lived in this stately brick house across the street from his linseed factory. *Courtesy of Thetford Historical Society.*

In the late 1800s, Samuel Saville was a cabinetmaker in Post Mills, and Hinckley spent time in his woodshop. Saville's daughter was a young girl who played in the shop and listened to conversations. The late Mary B. Slade wrote Wilbur Siebert in 1943 about Saville's daughter, a Mrs. Jacob, who shared that she "recalled hearing Dea. Hinckley as an old man, telling his adventures with the negroes."

Chelsea, Vermont resident John Comstock, whose wife was the granddaughter of Wilder Dearborn, the Chelsea agent, wrote to Wilbur Siebert in 1936, saying, "Negroes were brought to Chelsea by Lyman Hinckley, a Baptist deacon of Post Mills in the town of Thetford, and that they were taken on from here to Montpelier. This seems to be authentic. At any rate, it sounds reasonable. Post Mills is on the road which passes by the house

Lyman Hinckley, 1800–1885, was mentioned in numerous Underground Railroad texts as a friend of the slaves, always ready to help. He was a staunch Baptist and was respectfully called "Deacon Hinckley." He received fugitives from Lyme, New Hampshire, and hid them in his barn. Then he would transport them to the Chelsea safe house. *Courtesy of Thetford Historical Society.*

where Wilder Dearborn lived. This was about a mile from the village, to the east."

Lyman Hinckley was born in Post Mills around 1800, and his father, Joseph Hinckley, was originally from Connecticut. Joseph established the linseed oil factory, as well as the first and only mill in Thetford. In the 1800s, flax was a popular homegrown crop that was the source of the textile fibers woven into linen and cloth. A family could grow an acre of flax and weave enough to clothe themselves and use for exchange for other necessities. Also, the flax seed was the source of linseed oil used in paint and soaps. In 1846, Lyman took over the business, operating it for fourteen years. He sold the mill and was a farmer.

Lyman had four wives, with the first three dying young. Ann, his fourth wife, lived seventy-five years. Lyman had eight children. In the 1850 U.S.

Census, Lyman was registered as a forty-nine-year-old farmer and oilmaker. His household included wife, Anna, age forty; Lyman Jr., eighteen; Harriet, sixteen; Anna, three; and one-year-old twins, Charles and Amelia. He was recorded to have $3,600 in real estate.

He was a zealous Baptist who was instrumental in supporting the Post Mills Baptist Church. His reputation in the Baptist church outlived him, and even in his daughter Harriet Hinckley's 1892 obituary, it stated that she was the "daughter of Deacon Hinckley (Lyman) who for fifty years was identified with the Baptist cause in Vermont."

From the mid-1840s, Lyman was instrumental in the Post Mills Lyceum where local leaders met once a week to discuss national issues and share news updates.

He continued farming, even at eighty years old. Hinckley lived long enough to enjoy victory from the fruits of his labors in the fight for freedom, witnessing the Emancipation Proclamation. He died at age eighty-two in 1885.

CHELSEA

From Hinckley's house in Post Mills, fugitive slaves were taken to Wilder Dearborn's house in Chelsea. Dearborn, with the help of his son Franklin, took fugitives to Montpelier, a distance of about twenty-nine miles. Dearborn's farm was one mile east of Chelsea, past the High Bridge.

Wilder was born in 1794 in Chester, New Hampshire, and moved to Chelsea with his family when he was five. He built his house in 1820, and the old stagecoach route ran through his dooryard. In his great-great-granddaughter Elisabeth Burbank's research, it said that Wilder moved the house north and built a barn. Wilder was a farmer and a member of the Congregational Church. He served as selectman from 1829 to 1832 and later from 1846 to 1849.

In 2011, Burbank researched Wilder, her great-great grandfather, and wrote, "He was also involved with his son Franklin in providing a way station for the Underground Railroad."

John M. Comstock responded on February 14, 1936, to Siebert's query about an Underground Railroad station in Chelsea. His wife's father was Franklin Dearborn, who assisted his father, Wilder, in transporting runaways.

Comstock wrote, "My wife recalls that her father often spoke of his father's having harbored runaway slaves and passed them on to other stations.

Apparently this was not one instance alone, but was a repeated occurrence. I think then it may be safely set down that Wilder Dearborn, who died in 1855, was a regular agent of the Underground Railroad in Chelsea."

Comstock wrote a second letter to Siebert dated February 27, 1936, that there was confirmation from another son of Wilder Dearborn's, who shared that the "Negroes were brought to Chelsea by Lyman Hinckley, a Baptist deacon of Post Mills in the town of Thetford, and that they were taken on from here to Montpelier."

John Burbank of Bristol, Vermont, a descendant of Wilder Dearborn, said that there was a room called the "slave room" in the Dearborn house in Chelsea, just off the kitchen, but it was a regular room, not a hidden one. Burbank's grandmother was Hattie Hinckley Dearborn Burbank, the daughter of Franklin and Sylvia. Franklin inherited the Dearborn farm.

Burbank said in a 2013 interview, "As a child in the 1940s, I often visited my grandparents and heard about the slave room. It was the room with the window to the right of the end entrance door. Whether the station was still in operation after 1850 is not known and how many fugitive slaves might have passed through isn't on record either."

BRANDON

The famous Vermont 1793 court ruling known as the Dinah Matteis case defined Vermont's antislavery stance early in its history. Court was held in Brandon and Judge Theophilus Harrington ruled that in the state of Vermont, a Southern slave owner could not reclaim his two runaway slaves (Dinah Matteis was one). Harrington stated that "only a bill of sale from God Almighty" would make him hand over the two fugitives. Case closed, fugitives were free.

Rodney V. Marsh's home on Pearl Street in Brandon was known as a safe house for fugitive slaves. A *Rutland Herald* May 31, 1939 newspaper article titled, "Rodney Marsh Famous Home Is at Brandon" featured an interview of Rodney's son Edward. The article stated, "Many a dusky, trembling fugitive paused overnight near the end of his flight from the southland, to be given food and a place to sleep before proceeding once more on his journey."

Edward's father moved to Brandon in 1836. In 1852, he built one of the most ornate homes in town. Taking two years to build, the Marsh home had a maze of rooms, including more than fifty closets used for hiding, eight escape stairways from various floor levels and a tunnel connecting the cellar to the outdoors.

Edward told of his father's connection with the famous "Personal Liberty bill" for Vermont and described his work as chairman of the special committee on the Dred Scott decision. He stated, "Rodney Marsh did not confine his battle against slavery to the operation of his station of the 'underground.'" He fought in the Vermont legislature and in the papers and periodicals of the time. In 1850, Marsh was chairman of a legislative committee that drafted a resolution about the illegality of the Fugitive Slave Act of 1850.

In a November 25, 1858 *Green Mountain Freeman* article, Marsh's "untiring labors the report has been perfected, we have only to say that those who have known him and his long devotion to the cause of Freedom will not be disappointed in a careful perusal of the report. His name will be associated with those of Judge Harrington, Brainerd, Shafter, Slade, Fletcher, Needham, Roberts and a host of other worthy champions of freedom in Vermont."

Marsh sent fugitive slaves on to Chipman's Point, where they could board a boat bound for Canada, or he sent them to a Sudbury safe house.

Marsh died in 1872 and was eulogized by the famous poet John Greenleaf Whittier, who wrote to Marsh's widow, saying, "Thy husband's name was well known among anti-slavery folk beyond the limits of this state. The old pioneers of the good cause are fast passing away."

HARDWICK

I have seen in the "Emancipator" an account of a Bale of Cotton moving off from New Haven...
This Bale, after moving from place to place for about three weeks, rolled into my house last evening, and this morning, Started for the dominion of Victoria, where it is now safely stowed away.
—1843 letter by the Reverend Kiah Bayley in the Emancipator

Hardwick was a busy town with an antislavery society established in 1836 that, by the second year, had fifty-seven members. The most well-known operator was the Reverend Kiah Bayley, who worked with Montpelier minister Chester Wright running slaves from Montpelier to Hardwick.

Once in Hardwick, Bayley would hide them in the Stage House, a large two-story house next-door to his house. The Stage House has a hidden, five-sided room behind the chimney and also a tunnel under the house. Bayley may have utilized the unique hidden room in his neighbor's house instead of using his own home. From here, the fugitives were taken sixteen miles north to Albany.

The Reverend Kiah Bayley, 1770–1857, labored for the abolitionist cause, helping fugitives from Hardwick to Montpelier and lecturing about antislavery. Bayley's grave, in a Hardwick cemetery on Hardwick Street, refers to him as an "embassador of the Lord Jesus Christ." *Courtesy of Michelle Arnosky Sherburne.*

Bayley was born in Newbury, Vermont, in 1770 and was one of the first Newbury students to be accepted to Dartmouth College, graduating in 1793.

A year later, Bayley married Abigail (who was fourteen years his senior). He became a minister and took a pastorate in Newcastle, Maine, for twenty years. Bailey was the founder of the Bangor Theological Society and Lincoln Academy. He was president of the Maine Missionary Society, was instrumental in establishing Bowdoin College and was one of the founders of the American Board of Foreign Missions.

After twenty-seven years in the pulpit, in 1823, there was friction in the church, and Bayley resigned. The couple moved to Hardwick Street in Hardwick, which was populated mostly by his family. Bayley was fifty-six, and Abigail was seventy.

He served as pastor at the Congregational Society of Greensboro in 1825; in Thornton, New Hampshire, for two years; and then back to Hardwick. At this time, he and Abigail bought the house beside the Stage House.

Bayley then focused his energies on the abolitionist cause. He lectured about antislavery, preached sermons against slavery, wrote tracts and letters

Fugitive slaves were hidden by the Reverend Kiah Bayley, in a secret, five-sided room behind the chimney of the Stage House, built by Alpha Warner. The Stage House is next door to the Reverend Kiah Bayley's house on Hardwick Street in Hardwick. *Courtesy of Michelle Arnosky Sherburne.*

about abolition. Bayley and Wright were co-founders of the Caledonia County Antislavery Society.

Abigail died in 1846 at the age of eighty-nine, and Bayley sold the house and moved in with a local family. He continued his letter-writing campaign, and when the Fugitive Slave Law of 1850 passed, Bayley wrote and preached against it.

In a February 12, 1851 letter to educator Horace Mann, Bayley wrote about his own involvement in the Underground Railroad: "I assist a poor fugitive, as my conscience requires, and am persecuted. I appear before the courts, confess the fact, state that I have carried out my religion in so doing and appeal to the Constitution for my justification…The Fugitive Slave Law prohibits the free exercise of charity to the poor by pains and penalties."

Bayley died on September 15, 1857, at the age of eighty-seven years old.

MONTPELIER

Railroads and roads met at the capital city, making Montpelier an important center of Underground Railroad activity. There were several Underground Railroad safe houses and operators, but at the top of the list are Colonel Jonathan Miller and Joseph Poland.

Colonel Jonathan Miller

Colonel Jonathan Peckham Miller was born and raised in Randolph, Vermont. Not much is recorded about his childhood except that his father died when he was two. He enlisted with the Randolph volunteers for training in Plattsburgh, New York, probably during the War of 1812.

After that war, Miller enlisted in the army in 1817 and served for two years. Miller attended college in Burlington, but the college buildings burned in 1824. Miller was distracted from his studies by an interest in Europe—particularly Greece's fight for independence, which began in 1821. Because the American Revolution had inspired enslaved Greeks, they started sending out pleas for the United States to send aid to help them in their cause. This changed his life.

In 1824, Miller traveled to Greece, learned the language and joined the guerrilla fighters. He fought well and was fearless in battle, earning the nickname "The American Daredevil." He was promoted to colonel. Eventually, Miller's Greek freedom fighting days came to a close because it took a toll on him, and he returned to the United States.

But Miller's affiliation did not end because the Greek

This is a portrait of Colonel Jonathan Peckham Miller, a Montpelier Underground Railroad agent. *Courtesy of Vermont Historical Society.*

revolution raged on. Back in the States, he collected $17,500 worth of supplies, which he personally took back to Greece and distributed to the suffering civilian population.

After that trip, it was time to settle down. Miller married Sarah Arms in 1828 and settled in Berlin, Vermont, to raise a family. In 1831, Miller became a lawyer and opened his own practice. He also got involved with politics and was elected to the state legislature in 1831. Colonel Miller introduced a resolution in 1833 calling for Vermont's senators and representatives in Washington to promote the abolition of slavery and slave trade in the District of Columbia.

Miller devoted his time and money to the abolitionist cause. He lectured on abolition and coordinated abolitionist lectures in the state. He was immortalized for his role in crowd control at the 1835 Reverend Samuel May abolitionist lecture in Montpelier. Miller was one of two Vermont delegates to travel to London for the World's Antislavery Convention held in 1840. The Littleton, New Hampshire Anti-Slavery Convention was held in 1841 with speakers Miller, William Lloyd Garrison, *Herald of Freedom* editor Nathaniel Peabody Rogers and others.

Siebert wrote that Miller was "an earnest abolitionist, and deserves a high place in the annals of men who have sought to free the oppressed."

He took on the active role and helped slaves as an Underground Railroad operator in Montpelier. Area people knew that he helped runaways. Miller received many fugitives, and he transported them by wagon ten miles to the next depot.

His daughter Sarah Keith wrote Siebert in 1897 of her father helping fugitive slaves. Keith remembered fugitives were arriving at their house as early as 1837, when she was seven years old. Keith wrote: "These were often picked up along the road by drivers of the six-horse stagecoaches and were delivered at their door. When the colonel came out, the drivers were apt to tell him jokingly that they had brought some of his friends. He always thanked them for their kindness and ushered the newcomers into the house."

Miller worked for the antislavery cause up until his death in 1847, unfortunately not living long enough to see the culmination of the cause's work in the abolition of slavery.

Joseph Poland

Vocal proponent of abolition and active Underground Railroad operator Joseph Poland of Montpelier was a newspaper man who was responsible for several of Vermont's antislavery publications. He started in the newspaper business as an apprentice at the *Vermont Watchman* in 1835. Coincidentally, he witnessed the riot at the Reverend Samuel May's lectures in Montpelier that same year. The revelation about the reality of slavery set him on a course. His newspaper career gave him a voice for his newfound abolitionist beliefs.

By 1839, Poland, at age twenty-one, branched out on his own, establishing the *Voice of Freedom* with a partner. Poland turned ownership over to the Vermont Anti-Slavery Society, and it served as its mouthpiece.

Poland moved to Johnson, Vermont, and established another periodical, *Lamoille Whig*, which he ran for four years. In 1840, he got married and had seven children.

Joseph Poland of Montpelier was influential politically and in the media due to his lifetime of newspaper work. He was an Underground Railroad agent who shared firsthand knowledge of Vermont's network to help fugitive slaves. *Courtesy of Vermont Historical Society.*

The man was always busy with his work as well as community and civic duties. He was the judge of probate, member of the Senate, Montpelier representative in state legislature, Vermont State Library trustee, internal revenue collector, director and secretary of the Farmers' Mutual Fire Insurance Co. and a member of Bethany Church where he served as senior deacon and Sunday school superintendent.

He was a well-known friend of the fugitives, helping many through Montpelier. He didn't use his house for his Underground Railroad activities but rather used his office at 27 School Street by the courthouse, where the post office is today.

Wilbur Siebert corresponded with Poland directly, providing firsthand information about Vermont's Underground Railroad. In Poland's case, "secrecy in handling the fugitives was uncalled for" most of the time. In his office in Montpelier, Poland had a large closet that was convenient for hiding fugitives when it was necessary to hide them. He also stated that "scores and hundreds of runaways were received." Siebert learned from Poland how routes were established and known as trunk lines.

Jacob G. Ullery, author of *Men of Vermont: An Illustrated Biographical History of Vermonters and Sons of Vermont,* 1894, wrote highly about Poland, saying, "During his long residence in Montpelier, Judge Poland's political and personal influence has been far-reaching and effective, and has been freely sought and acknowledged in connection with most public men and measures of his time. Proverbially public-spirited, he has ever moved far in advance of men of much larger means in encouraging every business, benevolent, or social enterprise in his community; the sick and the suffering have always found in him a friend and benefactor; and the worthy young men are by no means few whom he has encouraged and assisted to enter upon a successful business career for themselves."

Poland returned to Montpelier in 1844 to establish yet another periodical, *Green Mountain Freeman.* This paper was the "organ" for the newly formed Liberty party. Poland was heavily involved with this successful venture, which he shared partnership of with his son, J. Monroe Poland.

Due to poor health, Poland sold the paper in 1849. In 1861, he was commissioned by President Abraham Lincoln to visit the Vermont regiments in the field to check on soldiers' pay and family subsidies.

Under a gubernatorial commission in 1863, Poland purchased the "Fair Ground" property now known as Seminary Hill in Montpelier and erected the buildings that made up the "Sloan Hospital," a hospital for Civil War soldiers run by the state.

Poland was tireless in his pursuit of journalism even in his old age. He published the *Vermont Chronicle* in 1875. Then he established the *New Hampshire Journal* in 1881.

St. Albans

St. Albans was a center of activity for Underground Railroad traffic, receiving runaways from the eastern New York routes into western Vermont. Siebert wrote, "Many fugitives were received and cared for here, and were sent on by private conveyance across the Canada border before the Vermont Central Railroad was built. Afterwards they were sent by rail, through the intervention of the Hon. Lawrence Brainerd, of St. Albans, who was one of the projectors of the steam railroad and largely interested in it financially." Lawrence Brainerd was well known for his leadership in the abolitionist cause, as well as in railroad and steamship business and political arenas.

Brainerd was born in East Hartford, Connecticut, in 1794. He was raised by an uncle and moved to St. Albans in 1808. By the age of twenty-two, Brainerd was running a successful mercantile business. Brainerd then got into the steamboat business on Lake Champlain. In 1847, he supervised the construction of the *United States*, a popular ship on Lake Champlain.

The St. Albans Underground Railroad agent was Lawrence Brainerd (1794–1870). He is buried in the Greenwood Cemetery in St. Albans, and his house still exists. *Courtesy of the University of Vermont Libraries, Special Collections, Bailey/Howe Library.*

He moved on to a new form of transportation in the Antebellum era—the railroad. He was instrumental in the construction of the Vermont & Canada Railroad and the Missisquoi Railroad. He was active in politics and was elected to the Vermont State legislature in 1834. He also ran unsuccessfully for governor.

His philanthropy extended into his involvement with the Underground Railroad as well as being an active member of the American Antislavery Society. He served American Antislavery Society manager from 1833 to 1839. Through the society, he made many connections in abolitionist circles.

Brainerd also believed in colonization for blacks and served as statewide chairman of the Vermont Colonization Society.

Ezra Brainerd shared information with Siebert that his father received word of fugitive arrivals in advance. Sometimes they were escorted by an agent to his home, and sometimes they arrived alone with credentials. With his waterway travel connections, Brainerd was able to send fugitives by water to St. Johns or Rousses Point. Brainerd's nocturnal guests were taken eighteen miles to Mancisco Bay, which stretched north into Canada.

In 1849, when the railroads were introduced to Vermont, Brainerd used the railroad for furthering fugitives to the Canadian border.

Brainerd's family was active in aiding in his Underground Railroad work. His wife, Fidelia, helped in his Underground Railroad efforts. Ezra became a famous botanist and president of Middlebury College. He later wrote about helping these fugitives when he was a boy: "Often these fugitive slaves were kept overnight at our house, and I was told to be up early and take them in our carryall [wagon]…The poor creatures seemed to suffer badly from the cold, and I recall hearing one of them pray 'Lord, don't let [me] freeze to death so near freedom!' When we reached the iron post that marked the Canada line they would all jump out and shout in ecstasy, 'Thank the Lord, now we'se freemen.'"

In *St. Albans, Vermont; Through the Years*, Brainerd was recorded as "a strong believer in the antislavery movement in this area, and his North Main Street home was part of the famed "Underground Railway" by means of which great numbers of slaves were able to escape from the South to safer ground in Canada."

Webster Kentucky Farm Association

Another facet of the antislavery cause Brainerd was involved in was the Webster Kentucky Farm Association (WKFA), the brainchild of Vergennes, Vermont native Delia Webster. The WKFA was a free-labor farm experiment in the slave state of Kentucky that Webster started. It was also a front for receiving and conveying runaway slaves for which Delia Webster was charged and arrested for numerous times.

Webster traveled east to fundraise for the association. Brainerd served on the board of directors as president. The association was active from 1858 to 1869, when Webster had to relinquish the property and the WKFA dissolved.

SWANTON

The Honorable William L. Sowles was a secret Underground Railroad agent who was also a prominent, wealthy citizen of Swanton. His home was in the center of Swanton Village facing the Village Green and across from the Congregational Church.

The North Country Underground Railroad Historical Association's website highlights a personal recollection of Samuel Boyd of Glens Falls, New York, from 1927 about his encounter with runaway slaves and Sowles. Boyd shared a story of his father delivering two runaways to Swanton.

> *Many of our prominent citizens knew all the ropes and helped pull them. A personal item here will explain something of the system. I went out one winter morning to feed our cow. When I went up to the hayloft I saw pushed out from under the hay a big pair of shoes and heard a powerful snore. To say I was frightened is putting it mildly. I rushed into the house and told father what I had seen and heard. I was straightaway set in a chair with the admonition not to say a word about it and not leave the room all day. Twice during the day I saw father take out food in a pail to the barn, and as evening darkened he drove in the yard with a long sleigh loaded with bags, opened the barn door and drove in. Then he came out, the load apparently the same. He was gone until the third day at night, when he came home. Meantime, I was told all about it, and so impressed that I never mentioned it until slavery was no more. Father had two slaves in that load, whom he delivered to a Center in Swanton, VT and the next trip landed them over the border into Canada.*

The Sowles house is well known for its architectural features and the 1870s renovations that were done by the Sowles family. In all the architectural, historical information about the Sowles house, the Underground Railroad factor is not mentioned. However, there is physical evidence in the house's two cellars. One is a small, shallow stone cellar beneath the kitchen ell with a concrete floor, and the second is a larger, deep brick one with two different floor levels beneath the main block of the house. The two cellars are connected by a crudely dug, brick-lined passageway with access to the passage through a small cellar behind a Victorian storage cupboard under the stairs.

Swanton is near Lake Champlain, not far from the Canadian border and only ten miles north of St. Albans. Sowles received fugitives and sent them eleven miles to Franklin, Vermont, to the home of Charles Felton.

Sowles was a well-known persona in Underground Railroad circles, but his work was not highlighted in any of his biographies. Just like Titus Hutchinson of Woodstock, his public life and Underground Railroad work did not collide.

Originally from Alburg, Vermont, one of the Champlain Islands, Sowles was a tradesman and farmer before entering the political arena in 1828. He was Alburg's representative and then served as Grand Isle County senator. In 1850, he was appointed as county court judge. He had five children with his wife, Alice.

While living in Swanton, Sowles was still involved in farming, working the land on large estates on the shores of Lake Champlain. He later became president of Union Bank and, in 1864, was president of Farmers Mutual Fire Insurance Company of Montpelier. Sowles died in 1878.

BURLINGTON

Reverend Joshua Young

I pronounce American Slavery to be a monstrous wrong, a heinous sin before High Heaven, provoking the righteous indignation of God, who will come in terrible judgment upon this nation, if we do not, away with it!
—The Reverend Joshua Young in an 1854 sermon

The Reverend Joshua Young, born in 1823, was a Massachusetts native who graduated from Bowdoin College and Harvard. He became a pastor at North Church in Boston's North End in 1849. Soon after, he married Mary Plympton.

While living in Boston, Young witnessed tumultuous events as the antislavery movement grew stronger. He experienced the injustice of the rendition of Thomas Sims and heard about the famous Shadrack rescue. Young became an impassioned advocate for the abolitionist movement. This led to his involvement in Underground Railroad efforts harboring fugitives while in Boston. He made many Underground Railroad connections in Massachusetts.

In 1852, Young was called to the Congregational Unitarian Church in Burlington, Vermont and moved his family north. He became close friends with one of his parishioners, Lucius Bigelow, an industrious young man and well-known abolitionist in Burlington. Soon, they were working together helping fugitives northward.

Young lived at the corner of Willard and College Streets, and across the street lived Salmon Wires, also an agent for the Underground Railroad. Working with Bigelow and Wires, Young received fugitives whenever he could. Different than his mode of operation in Massachusetts, he hid them in his barn.

Young was acquainted with Elizabeth Buffum Chase and other Underground Railroad agents in Valley Falls, Rhode Island. Chase and her husband received fugitives who had landed at Cape Cod and traveled to New Bedford. Mr. Chase would accompany them on the Providence and Worcester Railroad. He would place them in the care of a railroad employee who transferred them from Worcester, Massachusetts, north to the Vermont Railroad.

The wives of Young and Wires assisted in these efforts, coordinating the comings and goings of fugitives because it was less conspicuous for them to do it than for their husbands. The Youngs did not hide slaves in their house because of the public nature of his pastorate and the increased possibility of discovery.

The Reverend Joshua Young was active in aiding fugitive slaves in Burlington, and he officiated at the funeral of John Brown in North Elba, New York. *Courtesy of First Unitarian Universalist Society.*

In an 1893 letter to Siebert from Young, he stated, "A short period after the enactment of the Fugitive Slave Law of 1850 they came nearly every day singly, though sometimes in parties of two or three." He also wrote that normally the fugitive traffic was two or three every two weeks. He and Bigelow did "considerable business" aiding fugitives in Burlington.

In 1854, he traveled to Boston to see the capture and return to slavery of fugitive slave Anthony Burns. Young's trip angered some of his parishioners, but Young preached about it fervently when he returned, which further alienated many of his parishioners during his tenure.

He continued to raise the ire of his congregation by his antislavery preaching and the final blow to his Burlington career occurred after John Brown's funeral. After the 1859 execution of John Brown for the raid at Harper's Ferry, Brown's widow and an entourage traveled to North Elba, New York, to bury him. The funeral entourage made its way through the New England states and through Vermont, crossing Lake Champlain into New York State. Young and Bigelow decided to make the trip to attend the funeral, a decision that would affect Young's pastorate and future.

Wendell Phillips, a well-known Boston abolitionist and associate of William Lloyd Garrison, welcomed Young and Bigelow. Phillips enlisted Young to officiate at John Brown's funeral on December 8, 1859. Later in life, Young wrote an article about his role in the funeral that printed in the *New England Magazine* in 1904.

Afterward, Young and Bigelow returned to Burlington. Young felt a strong freeze immediately upon his return. The following Sunday, six prominent Burlington families left his church, and he was denounced by a Burlington newspaper for preaching at John Brown's funeral. By the end of December, Young had been socially ostracized, and he resigned again. The Youngs left Burlington and moved to Hingham, Massachusetts.

Young served as a minister for years, into his old age. In 1893, Young was living in Groton, Massachusetts, when Siebert contacted him about the Underground Railroad.

Lucius Bigelow

Lucius Bigelow's father, Lawrence, was a Vermont native who moved to Stanstead, Quebec, and ran lumber and mercantile businesses. Lucius was born in 1841 in Canada. Lawrence moved his family to Burlington around 1843. Lawrence was very active in the antislavery movement and was known in Burlington as a strong abolitionist. It was in this atmosphere that Lucius was raised.

When abolitionist and Underground Railroad agent Reverend Joshua Young came to Burlington in 1850, Lucius associated himself with the man. They worked together for the cause and helped fugitive slaves traveling through Burlington.

Siebert wrote in *Vermont's Anti-Slavery and Underground Railroad Record* that Bigelow was the principal Underground agent in Burlington. Siebert stated, "It seems to have been widely known in the town that Mr. Bigelow looked after such persons and many were directed to him." He received fugitives from as far as sixty miles away in Rutland. Wires and Young worked with Bigelow, and they shipped fugitives from Burlington on the Central Vermont Railroad to Canada.

Bigelow lived at 272 Church Street in a three-story colonial beside the home of another Underground Railroad agent, Reverend John K. Converse. Converse lived beside the Burlington Female Seminary. There was said to be a tunnel running from Converse's house to the seminary building. Bigelow used an ell in his house to hide fugitives. His house was close to the railroad tracks.

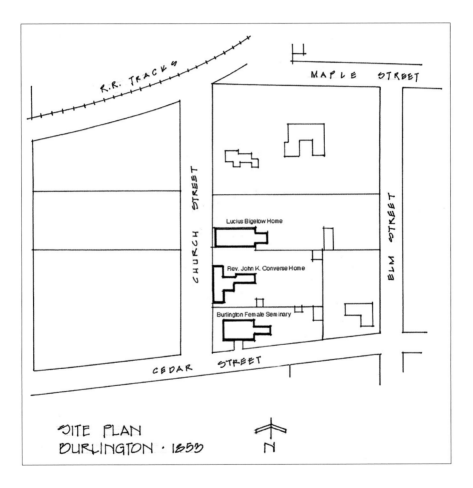

This rendition is of an 1853 Burlington map of the Church Street neighborhood, which had the Vermont Central Railroad tracks running through Church Street. Underground Railroad agents Lucius Bigelow and the Reverend John Converse were neighbors. The Burlington Female Seminary was on the corner of Church and Cedar streets, which was established by Converse. A tunnel is said to have run from the Converse house to the seminary for ease in moving fugitives. Bigelow's house had a hiding place in the ell, and he was the busiest Underground Railroad agent in Burlington. His house was under surveillance often, so having a backup plan next door helped. *Illustration by Charles E. Metz, architect.*

When the Civil War began, Lucius enlisted in August 1861 and served in the Fifth Infantry Regiment, Vermont's First Brigade. Bigelow was a sergeant and was mustered into service in September 1861. He served three years and was discharged on disability in 1863. He lived to see the fruits of his labors when slaves were freed. In 1878, Bigelow gave an oration before the Reunion Society of Vermont Officers in the House of Representatives Hall in Montpelier.

There were times when the Bigelow house was under surveillance and caution had to be exercised. One incident reported in Siebert's *Vermont's Antislavery and Underground Railroad Record* was about a foiled plan in which Bigelow and Wires planned to take fugitives by carriage to the next safe house. Due to the surveillance on his house, they devised another plot and were able to secretly get them to the train another way and board unnoticed.

Another time, Bigelow had six fugitives who had escaped from a Virginia plantation hidden in his shed. Bigelow went to Young for help. The fugitives were taken to Wires's office, where they collapsed on the floor and slept. Young supplied them with food and Wires got new clothes from the store of another abolitionist, Edward Peck. The next night, Wires and Bigelow drove the fugitives to St. Albans to get on the train to Montreal and freedom.

A forty-year-old fugitive woman arrived in Burlington in the middle of winter. She had escaped from her owner in Tennessee. Once in Vermont, she followed the railroad tracks from Rutland to Burlington. She stayed hidden once she reached the city of Burlington and then at night looked for Bigelow's house. She had been told who would help and how to find his house. She was in terrible physical shape, and Bigelow kept her at his home for three weeks until her health improved. Then he sent her on the way to Canada.

Reverend John Kendrick Converse

Lucius Bigelow's neighbor on Church Street was the Reverend John Kendrick Converse, also an Underground Railroad agent. Converse was a prominent colonizationist, whom Siebert wrote "aided fugitives and sometimes kept them until they were able to go on." Siebert wrote about an underground tunnel from Converse's residence to the seminary nearby for the safety of the fugitives.

In 1936, Siebert interviewed Burlington residents Abial Anthony and George Munson about Converse's role in the Underground Railroad.

Anthony, whose father, Tony Anthony, was a black Underground Railroad agent in Burlington, knew that Converse was an agent. Munson was told about the underground tunnel from the Converse house to the seminary by locals.

Converse was a Lyme, New Hampshire native who attended Dartmouth College and Hampden-Sidney College, graduating from the latter in 1828. He moved to Richmond, Virginia, to teach and help his brother with a newspaper before he returned north to study theology at Princeton Theological Seminary.

In the 1830s, he joined the American Colonization Society and served as a lecturer and fundraiser for the society in Vermont, New Hampshire, Maine and northern New York. Converse was involved with the Vermont Colonization Society, serving twenty-five years as its secretary.

It was in 1832 that Converse moved to Burlington to become the Congregational Church pastor. Two years later, he married Sarah Allen, a Burlington congressman's daughter. They moved to the Church Street house in 1844.

Converse saw a need in Burlington for a school for young women. There was none in the area, and wealthy parents had to send their daughters elsewhere for an education. Popping up all over the country, these popular schools, called female seminaries, taught young women finishing classes of art, music, philosophy and culture. Converse established the Burlington Female Seminary in 1844 with ten students that kept multiplying. The school was a success, and after three years, there were one hundred students, and Converse purchased additional buildings to accommodate the seminary. He served as principal, and there was a staff of teachers. Seminary students paid $140 per year for tuition and room and board. Over the thirty-six-year seminary history, three thousand women were educated at Burlington Female Seminary. Converse's health eventually failed, and he died in 1880. The school closed the same year.

In the November 1880 issue of *The African Repository*, a monthly publication of the American Colonization Society, there is a tribute to Converse and a reprint of his obituary. It reads, "A wide circle of acquaintances and friends will hold Mr. Converse in affectionate remembrance for his genial sympathies, his philanthropic labors, and his many Christian virtues."

The seminary building was believed to have hidden basement rooms for fugitive slaves and also a tunnel that led from the seminary to the Converse home.

Tony Anthony

Anthony was a free black cook in Burlington hotels and on steamboat kitchens on Lake Champlain. Because of this work, Anthony had access to the steamboats and hid fugitives on them, making sure they landed at St. Johns, Canada.

In the 1850s, he lived on Church Street, close to where the Holly brothers' boot shop was located.

Tony's daughters married free black men from the Hinesburgh Hill families: Jane married Loudon Langley, and Annette married George Williams.

Siebert reported that Tony's son Abial recalled seeing fugitive slaves in their house during the day but that they would be gone the next morning. Abial said that the fugitives were in their twenties and thirties, and he said he met some from Virginia and Louisiana.

Joseph C. Holly and James T. Holly

James and Joseph Holly were born free in Washington, D.C., and moved to Vermont in 1844 with their mother and sister. The Holly brothers had learned the shoemaking business from their father and opened a boot shop on Church Street in Burlington around 1849.

The brothers were on opposite sides of the antislavery fence, with James in favor of colonization and Joseph against it. The Holly family hosted debates about colonization.

Joseph was a regular contributor to Frederick Douglass's *North Star* publication. In 1851, he traveled to Boston and spoke at antislavery meetings.

James became a major leader in the colonization movement. He had a different perspective of colonization because he didn't think blacks would never be treated equally in the United States. He studied to be a teacher with fellow Underground Railroad agent Reverend John K. Converse in preparation to move to Liberia.

The Hollys' boot shop closed when the brothers went their separate ways. In 1851, James moved to Windsor, Canada, and worked with Henry Bibbs, the leader of the fugitive self-help movement. He was co-editor of the *Voice of the Fugitive* and wrote a book. By 1861, James helped lead 110 blacks to Haiti, as well as moving there himself. Joseph relocated to Rochester, New York, in 1851 but died shortly after in 1855.

HINESBURGH

Loudon Langley was a free black who grew up on Lincoln Hill in Hinesburgh, which was a small community of blacks. He aided fugitive slaves on occasion. He even mentioned assisting a fugitive in a letter to the *Green Mountain Freeman* in February 1855. It is also recorded that his parents, William and Almira Langley, aided fugitives on the Hill.

Langley was an abolitionist and was a constant letter contributor to the newspapers. He was strongly opposed to colonization. He wrote the *Freeman* in April 1855 that he didn't believe that any blacks in the Burlington area would even consider going to Liberia. He appealed to the public "to lend their influence with intent of giving us liberty and equal rights in the land of our birth."

When the Civil War began, Langley and two brothers enlisted in the famous Massachusetts Fifty-fourth Infantry. He was an advocate for enlisted blacks, fighting for their soldiers' pay. He wrote letters about the battlefront and sent them to the newspapers in Vermont. Langley kept Vermonters informed of what was happening on the front and the treatment of blacks in the service. He was adamantly against the unfair treatment of black soldiers and tried to get what was due them.

LISTING OF OTHER UNDERGROUND RAILROAD AGENTS

There is not enough room to dedicate a biography to every person in Vermont who had a connection to the Underground Railroad. But the following people deserve to be mentioned for their efforts:

Dr. S. Wilcox, Bennington
Dr. Eleazer Crain and son Henry Foster Crain, Springfield
Erastus and son Hervey Higley, Castleton
Simon Bottum family, Shaftsbury
Arhur Howard, Shaftsbury
Governor Richard Skinner, Manchester
Judge John S. Pettibone, Manchester
Benjamin D. Bowen, Felchville (now Reading)
John Sprague, West Windsor
Joshua Madison Aldrich, Weathersfield

Edmond Barrett, Hartland Four Corners
Asa Davis, Chester
Oramel Hutchinson, Chester
Reverend Joshua Clement, Post Mills
Reverend Standish D. Barnes, Montpelier
Reverend Jacob Seely, Montpelier
David E. Nicholson, Wallingford
Philbrook Barrows Jr., Wallingford
Lyman Batcheller, Wallingford
Stranahan family, St. Albans
Cyrus W. Wickers, North Ferrisburgh
Arian T. Ramsey, Brandon
R.R. Thrall, Rutland
Aaron and Dinah Rogers, Rutland
Daniel Roberts Jr., Burlington (also Manchester)
Mark Rice, Burlington
Samuel Huntington, Burlington
George Wyllis Benedict, Burlington
Reverend Alvah Sabin, Georgia
R.D. Fuller, Middlebury
E.D. Barber, Middlebury
Joseph Gordon, Middlebury
Frederick W. Kimball, Barton
Rev. George Putnam, Albany
Dr. Levi Moore, Troy
A.J. Rowell, Troy
David Camp, Derby
Portus Baxter, Derby
Professor James Dean, Nicholsen House, Burlington
Nicholas Guindon, Temperance Inn, Ferrisburgh
E.H. Converse, Charlotte
Daniel Woodward, Yuran-Sylvester House, Randolph
John Barrett, Barrett House, Grafton
Daniel Paddock, Bennington
Jonathan Dodge, Johnson
A.W.Caldwell, Johnson
Judge John M. Hotchkiss, Waterville
Col. Samuel Kendall, Enosburg
Andrew Comings, Berkshire

Reverend Green, Montgomery
Jefferson Martin, Montgomery
Dr. Arms, Waterbury
Deacon Butler, Waterbury
Deacon Parker, Waterbury
William P. Briggs, Richmond
E.A. Stansbury, Richmond
Amson Byington, Williston
William H. French, Williston
John Strong House, Addison
C.F. Thompson, Brattleboro
Oscar Shafter, Townshend
Hon. William R. Shafter, Townshend
D.E. Richardson, Wilmington
Lebbeus Edgerton, Randolph
William Perkins, Bennington
Ryland Fletcher, Cavendish

Dr. Thomas E. Powers lived in this house on Church Street, beside the Universalist chapel in the 1800s. He was an Underground Railroad agent and also owned an apartment building that housed blacks until it was destroyed by a local mob in 1835. *Photograph courtesy of the Woodstock Historical Society.*

Reverend Timothy P. Frost, Weston
Willard Frost, Brattleboro
John and Mary Clark, Rockingham
Reuben Fuller, Middlebury
Richard Carpenter, Bennington
Dr. S. Wilcox, Bennington
Fletcher Wright, Cavendish
Fessenden-Hanks House, Royalton
Sanford Granger, Bellows Falls
Charles Felton, Franklin
Simeon Parmalee, Pittsford
Madison Safford, Cambridge
Cyrus Prindle, Middlebury/Ferrisburgh/Shelburne
Samuel Chalker, New Haven
Elijah Alexander, Charlotte
Charles McNeil, Charlotte
Reverend John Wheeler, Burlington
Fernando Jacobs, Canaan

LISTING OF REPORTED VERMONT SAFE HOUSES

For so long, the emphasis on the Underground Railroad has been on the buildings used in the efforts and not the people who lived there. Hiding places, secret chambers, tunnels, trapdoors, staircase closets, fake walls, crawl spaces and hidden areas behind chimneys and in cellars still exist in old houses. Letters, diaries, records and documents are other forms of evidence. But it was the people who lived in the houses that we are interested in. Unfortunately finding owners during the 1820s to 1860s isn't always possible. These houses have been linked to possible Underground Railroad use.

Solomon Place and Three Pines Farm, Hartland
Clark-Martin House, Peacham
Heilman House, Manchester
Hildene Caves, Manchester
Douglas House, Taftsville
Zeicher House, Rutland
Golden Stage Inn, Proctorsville (Ludlow)

James Kinney House, Falls Road, Shelburne
Ellis-Brown House, Royalton
Whip Inn, Stowe Village
Sias House, Newport
John Strong House, Addison
Fessenden-Hanks House, Royalton
Bassett House, East Village, East Montpelier
Old Weeks Tavern, Bennington
Gay House, Windsor
Willard House, Hartland Four Corners
Porter House, Thetford Hill

The Chiselville covered bridge over the Roaring Branch brook in Arlington, Vermont, was a hideout for runaway slaves. In 1820, the town voted to have a way station or hostel built for escaped slaves on the Underground Railroad. *Courtesy of Michelle Arnosky Sherburne.*

Moses Swasey House, Newbury
Colonel Thomas Johnson House, Newbury
Hatch-Peisch House, Norwich
Warren Child's House, North Springfield
Stone Village *(This part of Chester had ten houses that were built around 1834 and used as a part of the Underground Railroad.)*
Jaquith House, North Thetford
Currier House, Berlin *(A pair of shackles from the 1800s were found in a cellar wall.)*
Farrington Homestead, Brandon
Bullard Inn, Swanton Junction

Chapter 6

NOTABLE VERMONTERS IN THE ABOLITIONIST MOVEMENT

Delia Webster: The Petticoat Abolitionist

Vergennes was the hometown of Delia Webster, Vermont's native daughter who had a lifetime mission to fight slavery. Webster made the history books as the first woman in the United States imprisoned for aiding a fugitive slave family, Lewis and Harriet Hayden and son, in Lexington, Kentucky, in 1844.

Born in 1817, she was one of ten children of Benajah and Esther Webster living in Vergennes. Benajah was a blacksmith and gunsmith. At an early age, Delia was a gifted teacher and began teaching fellow students. She constantly battled illness because of a weak constitution. By age twenty-two, her family sent her to Saratoga Springs, New York, to improve her health.

She left New England in 1841 to go to the abolitionist-based Oberlin College in Ohio. The college promoted Underground Railroad activity, and six routes ran through the campus. She made connections with abolitionists and Underground Railroad agents and learned from them. She was destined to be a woman in a man's world, not following the conventions of the day and expectations of young women her age.

Two years later, Webster was working with a married couple—the Spencers, whom she met at Oberlin—traveling around Ohio, Indiana and Kentucky. The trio established finishing classes to teach young women painting, literature and writing in different cities. They were teaching days, and their nights were free to make connections with slaves looking for escape

This was the Benajah Webster house on School Street in Vergennes where Delia Webster grew up. *Courtesy of Susan Ferland of Vergennes Historical Society.*

assistance. They made arrangements and facilitated the escapes. Time spent in each city was short so that their Underground Railroad work would not be discovered.

At the beginning of 1843, the Spencers and Webster arrived in Lexington, Kentucky, their next teaching target. They were accepted by the upper-class families and were encouraged to open a female seminary. In July 1844, the Lexington Female Academy opened. Within a month, the Spencers contracted high fevers and were forced to leave the hot climate. Webster was left alone to run the academy, but she was capable of handling the responsibility. She circulated the social scene and became involved in the community.

Her life changed drastically when she was contacted by a fellow Oberlin friend, Calvin Fairbank. Fairbank was a Methodist minister who had a reputation for slave rescues. He arrived in Lexington and stayed in the boardinghouse where Webster lived. In Siebert's *Underground Railroad: From*

The only photo in existence of Delia Webster is this original tintype. Delia Webster is pictured with her sisters in the front row on the left. *Back row, left to right:* Martha Webster Goodrich and Betsey Wilson Webster; *front row, left to right:* Delia Webster and Mary Jane Webster Bard. *Courtesy of Bard and Gina Prentiss, Dryden, New York.*

Slavery to Freedom and other texts like the Vermont Historical Society website, Webster is mentioned as a Vermont schoolteacher who accompanied Fairbank on the famous Lewis Hayden family escape. Her role was much more than a spectator. Webster was an accomplice and arranged the escape, using her Lexington connections to meet with Hayden.

On September 28, 1844, Webster and Fairbanks accompanied Hayden; his wife, Harriet; and son Joe in a carriage from Lexington to Ripley, Ohio, and on to the Underground Railroad to freedom. The Haydens escaped, ending up in Boston, where Lewis became a busy Underground Railroad agent and outspoken abolitionist.

It was discovered that there were missing slaves, and upon Webster and Fairbank's return to Lexington, the authorities and slave owners were waiting for them. A mob dragged Fairbank from the carriage, and he was beaten, tortured and kept in a basement cell of the Megowan Hotel, a makeshift jail. Webster was taken from her boardinghouse and lodged in a room in Megowan.

The experience from her September arrest until the December trial was fraught with interrogations, unfair treatment, captors' interception of correspondence and health problems. During her incarceration, Webster corresponded with her family, her Vergennes pastor and other New England abolitionists. She received support letters from Vermont authorities like Governor William Slade and legislator Samuel Phelps.

She was supported by her hometown, which rallied for her release. In Ferrisburgh, Underground Railroad agent Rowland T. Robinson led efforts to support their "Vermont daughter" in jail at antislavery meetings.

Two letters found in Fairbank's belongings spelled out the escape plans and described Webster's role in the escape. This incriminating evidence and a confession beaten out of the black carriage driver made a strong case against the two. They were put on trial separately. Webster's father arrived a week before her trial, which was held from December 17 to 21. She was convicted of "aiding and enticing slaves to leave their owners and to escape beyond the limits of Kentucky to Ohio."

Webster was sentenced to two years in the Kentucky Penitentiary. In February 1845, she began her prison term. She was befriended by the warden and his wife and was given a separate apartment from the other prisoners. Webster had a long visitor list of the upper-class people who missed her school.

Through serious negotiations by her father, the Kentucky governor pardoned Webster after serving only two months, though she was exiled from the state. She returned to Vermont with her father in March.

Meanwhile, Fairbank's trial was held and he was found guilty and sentenced to fifteen years in the Kentucky Penitentiary, five years per Hayden family member. Fairbank served his entire term, and his time in prison was horrible.

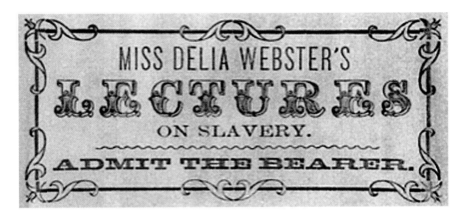

Delia Webster was on the abolitionist lecture tour throughout New England. This admission ticket to "Miss Delia Webster's Lectures on Slavery" is in a private collection. *Courtesy of Bard and Gina Prentiss, Dryden, New York.*

Within a month of Webster's Vermont return, she wrote the required apology pamphlet, a condition of her pardon. In April 1845, Webster's father paid for the publication of the pamphlet, "Kentucky Jurisprudence, A History of The Trial of Miss Delia A. Webster at Lexington, Kentucky, Dec'r 17–21, 1844, Before the Hon. Richard Buckner, On a charge of aiding Slaves to escape from that Commonwealth—with Miscellaneous Remarks, including her views on American Slavery, written by herself."

She was the top story for two years in the New England abolitionist media—"the woman who went to jail for slaves"—which generated support for the abolitionist cause. The pamphlet also caused much controversy among abolitionists who criticized Webster's pamphlet comments.

New England abolitionists didn't realize it was a pardon requirement and was intended to ingratiate Webster back into the good graces of Kentuckians. Her future goals would depend on her return to Kentucky, so she had to redeem herself to gain their forgiveness and trust.

There was also a difference in terms of what an abolitionist was in a slave state versus a free state. In Kentucky, Webster was considered a kidnapper and slave stealer for helping fugitive slaves. Kentuckians also called all abolitionists—Underground Railroad agents or not—"slave stealers." Webster wrote in her pamphlet that she denied "stealing and seducing slaves to run away," which confused New Englanders. She had to explain that she did "aid, help and assist" runaway slaves, but she denied Kentucky's terms of "seducing, enticing and kidnapping" runaway slaves. Kentuckians did not believe that slaves were capable of desiring to escape, thinking that they had to be tricked and brainwashed to run away.

In a *Filson Club History Quarterly* article by J. Winston Coleman Jr., he wrote, "Until the early forties, however, they had experienced little or no trouble with that much-despised class, scornfully known as 'nigger stealers' or 'agents' of the mysterious and powerful Underground Railroad." Coleman referred to Fairbank and Webster as "anti-slavery zealots" who were planning the "abduction of Negroes."

Another issue Northern abolitionists had with Webster were letters published during her incarceration. She spent three years fighting a war of words in the abolitionist newspapers and at conferences defending her letters and her actual abolitionist stands.

Her letters were questioned, scrutinized and debated. Abolitionists did not realize that every letter was censored by her captors so she used codes and double meanings. She defended herself from 1845 to 1847, writing to newspapers explaining that the letters "were private communications addressed to individuals who for a long time had known my sentiments too well to be deceived." She explained that Vergennes pastor Reverend Harvey Leavitt received these letters and, aware of her Underground Railroad activities, could read between the lines and understand her doublespeak.

The media war with Webster took a lot of time and energy. She was busy teaching, lecturing and traveling around New England. It took its toll, and she had to leave Vermont when her health failed. Webster moved to New York and opened a window shade business there. All the while, she corresponded faithfully with people in Kentucky and in 1846 received an invitation to return. Her efforts had paid off, and people in Kentucky and neighboring Indiana were ready to support her, with one notable supporter being the penitentiary warden, Nelson Craig.

By 1849, Webster had moved to Madison, Indiana, across the Ohio River from Kentucky. She was hired as a governess for Nelson Craig's children and spent a few years living and traveling with them. She made trips back to Vermont with the Craig children when she visited her family. Her relationship with the Craigs got her back into the social circles, and she made connections that would help later on.

When the pieces of her plan aligned, Webster broke away from the Craig family. She traveled East and made the rounds among the antislavery societies and abolitionist circles to raise money for her project. Back in Madison, Webster bought a home in town. She worked for over a year and purchased a six-hundred-acre farm with a few financial partners in Trimble

County, Kentucky, across the Ohio River from Madison. She established a free-labor farm with German immigrant workers in a slave state. The farm was productive with orchards, vegetable crops and cattle. It was also a front for an Underground Railroad safe house on the Ohio River.

After only six months, area slaves turned up missing. Slaveowners had lost approximately $30,000 worth of slaves who had run away. They couldn't prove that Webster was guilty, so they used other means to try to stop her. From 1853 to 1868, she executed her farm plans and Underground Railroad activity.

Neighboring slave owners despised her. Kentuckians now considered her evil and a demon and taught their children to fear her. They held meetings to attempt to eliminate her, and mobs raided her property, threatened her life and drove her off her own farm. She was exiled numerous times, fleeing to her Madison location in its free state status. She also frequently traveled back to New England to fundraise for her farm.

Craig held a grudge against her, so he used his legal connections to have arrest warrants issued for her and led numerous raids on the farm. She had a long history of fighting the authorities who tried to corner her, legally or otherwise. She was arrested, endured trials and served more jail time and even had to use the Underground Railroad herself to escape arrest.

At a Bedford, Kentucky town meeting in February 1854, a resolution was passed that stated: "Whereas it is known that Miss Delia A. Webster had recently run off numerous slaves from Trimble county, therefore resolved that it is the will and determination of the citizens of said county that Miss Delia A. Webster leave the State."

On June 26, 1854, Kentucky governor Lazarus Powell issued a warrant for Webster's arrest to the governor of Indiana. It stated: "Whereas, Delia A. Webster stands charged—indictments in the Fayette Circuit Court State of Kentucky with conducing and (enticing) away slaves from the possession & services of their masters and (overseers)...And whereas, information has been received at the executive department of this State, that the said Delia A. Webster has fled from justice and is now ___ (lodged) in the State of Indiana and it be important and highly necessary for the good of society that the perpetrators of such offenses should be brought to justice...demand the said Delia A. Webster as a fugitive from the justice of the laws of the State."

Webster now could not return to her Kentucky property because of the arrest warrant. She resided across the river in Madison and ran her farm from there.

The saga dragged on every year she operated the farm. The locals in Madison even tired of the Webster headlines and gossip. A letter to the editor in the *Louisville Democrat* of July 18, 1854, is titled "Delia Webster's Difficulties." It stated:

> *Miss Delia A. Webster is still continuing to keep the citizens of this place and immediate vicinity in a state of ferment…I fear her unquiet disposition and the warmth with which she cherishes the one great idea, with her, of negro emancipation, will never allow her to become a good and peaceable citizen or neighbor of a Slave State…It would be a great blessing to the people of this section of the country if Miss Webster were to leave, and go to one of the most Northern States and remain there. We are all getting heartily tired of this continual turmoil and excitement about her. She has been repeatedly requested by the people of this community, as well as the people of Kentucky, to retire from our midst and let us remain in peace;… but her perverse disposition prompts her to stay amongst us, to be a source of continual excitement and difficulty.*

In 1858, Webster thought if she separated herself from the farm it might relieve some of the tension and persecution. So she formed the Webster Kentucky Farm Association (WKFA) with support from New England abolitionists to keep the farm going. She established a board of directors and acted as a silent partner. On the WKFA board of directors were New York Underground Railroad operator Lewis Tappan and St. Albans Underground Railroad agent Lawrence Brainerd as president.

Back East, Webster recruited thirty Massachusetts families with the help of Governor Nathaniel Prentiss Banks to move to Kentucky to work on the WKFA farm. The families traveled West with Webster, accompanied by farm equipment, in 1859. The WKFA was in operation from 1859 to 1866, though it faced constant persecution, property destruction, arrests, raids and legal issues.

During the Civil War, Webster volunteered as a nurse alongside her friend Harriet Beecher Stowe helping soldiers. Her farm was still operating though the Underground Railroad efforts came to an end when the Emancipation Proclamation was issued, freeing the slaves.

Webster and her farm continued to face persecution, and the property was burned in 1866 by a mob. She finally relinquished the property in 1869, and the WKFA dissolved.

She lived in Indiana, Wisconsin and Iowa. She taught blacks and poor children and returned to teaching her finishing classes. She spent thirty years living with her sister's family and her niece. In her golden years, she wrote tons of letters about the injustices of the world. She died at age eighty-six on January 18, 1904, in Des Moines, Iowa.

She never wrote an autobiography about her life. Delia never bragged about her own Underground Railroad rescues, only citing the injustices of slavery in her writing. She made alliances to further her projects and had influential friends like Harriet Beecher Stowe, Calvin Fairbank, John and Mary Preston, Cassius Clay, Lawrence Brainerd, Lewis Hayden and Lewis Tappan.

In Trimble County, Kentucky, she was known as the "Petticoat Abolitionist," and there is an historical marker honoring her work: "Underground railroad station, a mile west, run by Delia Webster on land bought with funds provided by Northern abolitionists, 1854. Slaveholders filed charges against her. After refusing to leave Ky., she was imprisoned. Following her release she was indicted again but escaped into Indiana. For similar activities in Lexington she had served term in penitentiary, 1844."

Her controversial, tumultuous life was played out in the media at the time, but Webster is not well known in New England today. She was a heroine who was self-reliant and focused on her self-appointed mission to fight slavery and educate the poor. She was a unique gem.

WILLIAM SLADE

Middlebury native William Slade was an outspoken abolitionist. Although there isn't evidence he worked in the Underground Railroad, he fought slavery on state and national levels.

He was a prolific writer and published several books and pamphlets. He also established a newspaper in 1813. He entered the political arena in 1815 and began a long career in politics. Slade served as assistant judge of county court, clerk of Supreme Court for the county and clerk of the State Department in Washington. He spent five years with the State Department, and then Slade returned to Vermont to practice law for a while. But he couldn't stay away from politics. Slade served as Vermont's representative in Congress from 1831 to 1843, before moving to Washington again.

While in Washington, Slade was extremely vocal against slavery. In January 1840, he delivered a passionate speech calling for immediate emancipation, which was the first call made in the legislature, angering Southerners in the House. Garrison's *Liberator* called Slade "the first champion of immediatism in Congress."

He returned home in 1843 but not to a quiet existence. Slade was elected governor of Vermont for two years. Even as governor, Slade was not afraid to continue fighting against slavery.

Interestingly enough, one of his gubernatorial addresses was published and read by Lewis Hayden, a slave in Kentucky, who credited Governor Slade for inspiring him to seek freedom. Hayden and his family escaped from slavery in September 1844 with the help of Vermonter Delia Webster and Reverend Calvin Fairfield, both of whom were arrested. The Haydens made it safely out of slave territory and settled in Boston, where Hayden was instrumental in the Underground Railroad there.

After Slade's term was over, he devoted himself to education, serving on the Board of Popular Education, which recruited teachers to go west into newly formed states.

He died in Middlebury in 1859 at the age of 73, and didn't live long enough to see the end of slavery.

Always a public figure and a voice for antislavery, Slade made a permanent statement that would be read forever in the West Cemetery in Middlebury. On one side of Slade's cemetery monument, there is a memorial to a teenage girl, Eliza Dodson. It reads, "In memory of Eliza Dodson, colored, born in the City of Washington, Died April 19, 1853, Aged 18. Given by her mother to Wm. and Abigail Slade at the age of 7, a faithful, conscientious, devoted servant."

Slade and his family were living in Washington, D.C., while he was serving as senator. Washington was part of the slave states at the time, and Eliza's mother gave her to the Slades in 1842 at the age of seven. Slade's term ended the following year, 1843, when the Slades returned to Vermont. The Slades were not slave owners but did have servants while in the capital city. It seems reasonable to think that Eliza's mother wanted to get her daughter out of a slave state. It isn't clear if Eliza's mother went with them. Unfortunately, Eliza died young, and Slade must have regarded her as special since he chose to memorialize her on the Slade family monument.

Slade made a bold statement in 1853 by choosing to share his cemetery monument with a black person. He was a prominent Vermonter practicing what he preached in the halls of Congress—equality for all.

OLIVER JOHNSON

Oliver Johnson, a native of Peacham, was a noted abolitionist and dedicated his life to the cause, campaigning alongside his close colleague and mentor William Lloyd Garrison.

He was born in Peacham in 1809 and raised by a religious and abolitionist father who was a faithful subscriber to Garrison's first newspaper, the *Free Press*. His older brother, Leonard Johnson, was an Underground Railroad agent in Peacham and outspoken about his antislavery beliefs.

Oliver was educated at Peacham Academy and left home at sixteen to learn the printing trade at the Montpelier newspaper the *Watchman*. While in Montpelier, he heard Garrison lecture on emancipation and was converted to the abolitionist cause.

He lived in Middlebury while a resident of Vermont and was one of the founding members of the Vermont Anti-Slavery Society. Then he moved to Boston, New York and Pennsylvania while working in the antislavery newspaper business.

In 1831, Johnson established the *Christian Soldier* in Boston, next to where Garrison was printing. Johnson got his first taste of public speaking in his

The Leonard Johnson house was a station on the Underground Railroad on the Peacham-Danville Road in Peacham. Leonard Johnson also hosted abolitionist lecturers in his home, including his famous abolitionist brother Oliver Johnson, William Lloyd Garrison, Charles Bruleigh and Parker Pillsbury when they were on the lecture circuit in Vermont. *Courtesy of Neil and Jan Monteith private collection.*

home state when he lectured in Montpelier at the Congregational Church. He gave a strong speech about the evils of slavery and pushed for immediate emancipation. He was on his way.

Living in Boston, he surrounded himself with abolitionists and was part of the "Boston Clique" of Garrison, Wendell Phillips, Lydia Maria Child, Maria Weston Chapman and the Reverend Samuel May. It was a tight-knit group, and they supported each other in the cause. He also was involved in the establishment of the New England Anti-Slavery Society in 1832. Johnson worked with Garrison on *The Liberator* in 1840 and traveled with him.

When he relocated to Pennsylvania, Johnson was one of twelve organizers of the American Antislavery Society and served on the Philadelphia Anti-Slavery Society executive board in 1851. While living in Pennsylvania, Johnson was a regular correspondent to Vermont Underground Railroad agent Rowland T. Robinson about the abolitionist cause and, more importantly, about fugitive slaves he was sending to Robinson. Those Johnson letters are in the Rokeby Museum collection and were dated 1835, 1837 and 1840, when the Robinsons had a large amount of fugitive slave traffic.

During his newspaper career, he served as editor of antislavery newspapers *Standard* and *Christian Union,* as well as the *New York Tribune* and *New York Evening Post.*

He was a stalwart champion of the abolitionist movement, and in *Henry Ward Beecher: An American Portrait,* well-known abolitionist Henry Ward Beecher described him as "a wheel horse in every humanitarian movement for almost half a century, a man whose philosophy of life was quite simply to love his neighbor as himself."

Johnson was an early supporter of President Abraham Lincoln and organized a delegation to present the president with arguments about immediate emancipation. Johnson stated, "Let the union die if it must be reconciled to the sin of slavery in order to live, but the abolitionists could do the one thing to save its life by extirpating the cancer of slavery."

He dedicated his life to the abolitionist cause, either through media, speeches or helping fugitives on the move. He also wrote the book *William Lloyd Garrison and His Times; Or Sketches of the Anti-Slavery Movement in America,* printed in 1881, eight years before Johnson died.

THADDEUS STEVENS

Thaddeus Stevens is a nationally known historic figure who fought the slavery institution in Congress, was instrumental in the Thirteenth Amendment abolishing slavery and was an antislavery champion in Pennsylvania. Peacham and Danville, Vermont, both have claims on the famous "Great Commoner" who kept Congress on its toes during the 1840s and 1850s. Stevens was born in Danville, raised and educated in Peacham and spent his life working in Pennsylvania in politics and in the courtrooms.

Stevens's father deserted the family when Thaddeus was fifteen. His mother moved her four sons to Peacham. Childhood was difficult for him, growing up poor and helping support the family. He also suffered from a clubfoot, but he never let it slow him down. Stevens worked hard and excelled at everything he did. He graduated from the Peacham Academy and attended Dartmouth College. After graduation, he moved to York, Pennsylvania, for a teaching position. He taught during the day and studied law at night.

He opened a law practice in 1816 in Gettysburg and then moved to Lancaster, Pennsylvania, in 1842. Stevens entered the political arena in 1833 and was a strong antislavery force first in the Pennsylvania legislature and

A Vermont historical marker on the Danville Green commemorates the birthplace of Thaddeus Stevens, famous abolitionist, congressman and Underground Railroad agent in Pennsylvania. *Courtesy of Michelle Arnosky Sherburne, Vermont Division of Historic Sites, Roadside Historical Marker Program.*

then later in the U.S. House of Representatives as a congressman. Early in his career, Stevens handled numerous court cases, defending free blacks or fugitive slaves. He offered his legal counsel free of charge.

Stevens also aided fugitives on their way through the towns he lived in. Siebert wrote about him aiding fugitive slaves himself in Gettysburg and then in Lancaster. Siebert wrote: "His removal to Lancaster in 1842 did not take him off the line of flight, and he continued to act as a helper."

In 2003, archaeologists excavating a cistern on the Thaddeus Stevens property in Lancaster found a patched hole in the cistern wall. The hole was connected to a filled tunnel, and they located a patched doorway to an adjacent building on Stevens's property. It was theorized that people were sent from the building through the tunnel into the cistern as an emergency hiding spot.

A fifty-two-page narrative by fugitive slave Oliver Cromwell Gilbert was discovered in an antique shop in 2011. Gilbert's account states that his group was sent from Stevens to the home of Daniel Gibbons in Bird-in-Hand, Pennsylvania, a well-known Underground Railroad stationmaster. Gilbert wrote that slaves were told "to go to Lancaster and find an attorney at 45 South Queen Street who was a friend to the slaves."

Stevens was instrumental in the historic Christiana Riot trial in 1851. Thirty-nine people—fugitive, free, black and white—were on trial for the murder of slave owner Edward Gorsuch. With a small posse, Gorsuch had tried to reclaim his runaway slaves, pursuing them to a farmhouse in Christiana, Pennsylvania. A group of blacks and whites fought his posse, killing Gorsuch in the process. Thirty-nine were arrested and tried, but Stevens won the case for them, despite the new Fugitive Slave Law of 1850.

Politically, Stevens was a tough opponent in Congress and was relentless in his quest for abolition. He angered many Southern representatives because he didn't mince words about his abolitionist beliefs. He was nicknamed the "Great Commoner" and was hated by opponents. He was in the House of Representatives from 1849 to 1853.

He pushed President Abraham Lincoln to issue the Emancipation Proclamation and was instrumental in promoting the Thirteenth Amendment to abolish slavery. He was the chief framer of the Fourteenth Amendment, which provided equal treatment for all American citizens, and after the Civil War, he championed the Reconstruction efforts and wasn't lenient toward the South.

On the flip side, Stevens was a kind, generous philanthropist his entire life. He kept his ties to Vermont, supporting his mother as well as donating money to the Peacham Academy and the Peacham Library.

This is an illustration of Thaddeus Stevens posing an argument in Congress. *Public domain.*

Education was another focus of his, and Stevens pushed for public education in Pennsylvania, earning him the title "savior of public education." In his will, Stevens left $50,000 to establish a school for orphans that eventually became the Thaddeus Stevens College of Technology. Today, there are eleven schools that have been named in honor of Thaddeus Stevens in Washington, D.C.; Kansas; Vermont; and Pennsylvania.

He started an iron foundry in Gettysburg called Caledonia, after the county he was born in. During the Civil War, right before the Battle of Gettysburg, the forge was destroyed by Confederate general Jubal Early. Early destroyed it in retaliation of Stevens's well-known hostility toward Southern slave owners.

He died in 1868 and was buried in Lancaster, Pennsylvania, in a biracial cemetery. His self-composed epitaph reads, "I repose in this quiet and secluded spot, not for any natural preference for solitude. But finding other cemeteries limited as to race by charter rules I have chosen this that I might illustrate in my death the principles which I advocated through a long life, equality of man before his creator."

Chapter 7

UNDERGROUND RAILROAD LOCAL TRADITION AND PHYSICAL EVIDENCE

Local tradition plays an important role in discovering the history of the Underground Railroad. Information isn't always written down, but it is passed along verbally. The history of a town can be pieced together by the information that residents know and remember. In the quest for finding connections to validate Underground Railroad activity, we have to take into consideration the local tradition in reference to fugitive slave traffic in a town. If one can connect a reference of sending a fugitive slave to a particular town and learn that there is a house there that locals say was used on the Underground Railroad, and the 1800s owner's personal history reveals facts that could link him to the Underground Railroad, then it is the basis of a theory. It doesn't make it documented proof or fact, but it also cannot be easily dismissed.

When you can connect local tradition and physical evidence to an Underground Railroad incident, it is important not to dismiss the oral history just because it isn't documented in writing.

It is important to take into account how information is and was passed along in Vermont. If someone asked about runaway slaves, they might get an answer if the Vermonter trusted that person. If they weren't asked, then it wouldn't be shared. Decades ago, the subject of aiding runaway slaves was a taboo topic that wasn't talked about. Today, when a native Vermonter is asked, the information is shared and often is accompanied by a verbal footnote that people didn't talk about it back then. That's Vermont.

Vermonters have never been self-promoters, and native Vermonters don't share information readily with outsiders. In most cases, people didn't elaborate on their roles helping fugitives. In this state, things are better left alone, residents don't draw attention to something if it's bad and there are certain subjects that Vermonters refuse to discuss.

In Vermont, oral history is woven into the fabric of small towns because families have been there for generations. Small-town history isn't always written but shared verbally in Vermont. That becomes a problem when researching a subject or when historians want documentation. Just as the African American oral history is accepted, so too should Vermont's oral history.

A good example is when Wilbur Siebert interviewed Vermonter Mary Hatch about the Underground Railroad, and she shared stories she was told not to talk about as a child. Hatch wrote about her grandfather, John Sprague of West Windsor, and said that she stayed with her grandparents when she was six. One time, her grandfather returned to the house after working in the upper hay barn.

> *He came into the kitchen and said some thing to Grandma. She got a small basket and put bread & Butter & Cakes &c in it. I begun to ask why Grandma toled* [sic] *me little girls dont ask to many Questions and Grandpa went of with the basket, then when I was 15 years old I stayed with my Grandpa & Grandma a year…Grandma toled me that Grandpa found a big Negro asleep on the Hay up on the Schafold* [sic] *as it was caled and he cared the Basket and set it in the middle of the floor, the next day the food was gone and the man to and a few days after 3 men came out from Windsor 2 from Virginia and 1 of Windsor they were after run away slaves and they threatened Grandpa but did not scared him. I dont know that he ever had other Slaves but he mighed* [sic] *have.*

Researching local history is connecting the oral history, documented information and stories about towns and people. Piecing together those different interviews and information, a pattern forms and the places connect. Local history collaborates with other texts that mention these places.

When physical evidence exists, it needs to be examined. Why was this feature in this house? What could it have been used for? Are there connections to Underground Railroad use? Who was living in the house during the Underground Railroad timeframe, and did they have abolitionist background or a personal history that hasn't been revealed yet? Factors have to be taken into account to figure out if there is a connection. Sometimes the pieces fall in place and local tradition backs up the physical evidence, and if you are fortunate, somewhere there is documentation to back it up.

There are safe houses in Vermont that have the components that add up to Underground Railroad activity: physical evidence, local history, oral tradition and abolitionists.

BARNET

In Barnet, local tradition is that the Goodwillie House, owned today by the Barnet Historical Society, was a stop on the Underground Railroad, only three days away from the Canadian border.

The Goodwillie House is one of the oldest houses in Barnet, built by Reverend David Goodwillie in 1791. He and his son, Reverend Thomas Goodwillie, served consecutive terms in the Presbyterian Church for a total of eighty years. They shared livelihoods, and both lived in this house.

Stories of authorities coming to the Goodwillie House and checking for runaways have been passed down in Barnet history. Barnet historian David Warden said that "slaves would be hidden" in the secret brick enclosure behind the chimney base.

Reverend J.C. Hand, the 1992 caretaker of the Goodwillie House, said, "They would give them food and water. The runaway slaves were three days from freedom here in Barnet but were still apprehensive."

The physical evidence exists in the basement, where a hidden, brick compartment is concealed behind a fake stonewall next to the base of the chimney structure. This brick compartment is where runaway slaves were hidden.

The Goodwillie House, circa 1940, in Barnet. *Courtesy of the Barnet Historical Society.*

In the basement of the Goodwillie House, owned by the Barnet Historical Society, there is a brick enclosure that was built in the 1830s. To access the compartment hidden behind a stone wall and the chimney base, one has to crawl through this hole into the brick enclosure. The hiding space is standing room only, ten feet wide and seven feet high, and it runs twenty feet to the outside wall. *Courtesy of Michelle Arnosky Sherburne.*

During the 1800s, the original front entrance of the house was where the back of the house is today. The road originally passed right by the south side of the house, and the main entrance was via the door at the foot of the basement stairs that divided the three-room basement.

In the front cellar room, the chimney base is to the right and the fieldstone fake wall runs from the base to the stairwell wall. On the opposite side of the chimney base, there is a brick enclosure that was added around 1830. This enclosure is approximately twenty feet long, ten feet wide and seven feet high—a narrow, "standing room only" space. The only access to the brick enclosure is from the front room. One could not see the brick enclosure from the front room unless a large fieldstone was removed from the fake stone wall to open up to the brick hiding place.

Warden said that in 1950, he remembers when the fake wall was intact. He recalls a large fieldstone that could be pulled out, and you could see the hiding space. But then a neighbor kid pulled out some of the wall stones, and part of the fake wall collapsed. Now you can see the entrance to the enclosure and space between the brick wall and chimney base.

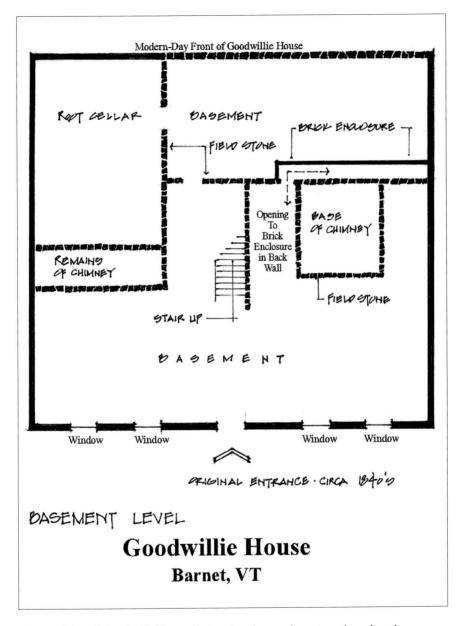

ROOT CELLAR BASEMENT

FIELD STONE

BRICK ENCLOSURE

Opening To Brick Enclosure in Back Wall

BASE OF CHIMNEY

REMAINS OF CHIMNEY

FIELD STONE

STAIR UP

BASEMENT

Window Window Window Window

ORIGINAL ENTRANCE · CIRCA 1840's

BASEMENT LEVEL

Goodwillie House
Barnet, VT

This rendition of Goodwillie House displays the nineteenth-century view when the modern-day back of the house was the front and faced the old road. The brick enclosure was concealed with a fieldstone wall that had an entrance stone that could be removed to gain access. Fugitive slaves came through the front door, which was on the basement level in the 1840s, and were directed to the enclosure beside the base of one of the chimneys. *Courtesy of Charles E. Metz, Architect.*

ST. JOHNSBURY

In 1837, an antislavery society was organized in St. Johnsbury. At the same time, sixteen other towns had formed their societies. St. Johnsbury surfaced on the list of Vermont towns that had a station of the Underground in Siebert's research. But was there no operator?

The station Siebert referred to was operated by Captain James Ramsey, who lived on the corner of Railroad Street and Concord Avenue. In the *Town of St. Johnsbury, Vt.*, by Edward T. Fairbanks, Ramsey is referred to as "a stiff antislavery man. His house was one of the underground railway stations, so called, where runaway slaves were taken in and helped on their way to Canada."

St. Johnsbury natives knew the Ramsey house was an Underground Railroad stop from stories passed on. An April 18, 1930 *St. Johnsbury Republican* article pointed out an interesting feature of the house: "Instead of having one cellar…it has two, a stairway leading down from the first to the second cellar. The bank on the side of the Main Street entirely covers any evidence of the second cellar. It was in this lower compartment of the house that the runaway slaves were hidden until nightfall."

In Claire Dunne Johnson's book *I See By the Paper...*, she wrote, "Capt. Ramsey was a man of strong convictions. He felt strongly against slavery and some of his neighbors suspected his house was a station on the Underground Railroad…This suspicion, which persisted down through the years, was proven correct in 1930, when that old house was torn down to provide the site for Woodbury & Benoit's garage. There, below the usual cellar, was another cellar area with no windows—a completely safe hiding place for Negro slaves trying to make their way to freedom."

The late Graham Newell, who grew up in St. Johnsbury, said in a 1992 interview, "My father pointed out the Ramsey house every time we went by and told me that the building was an Underground Railroad stop. I was in the eighth grade when it was being torn down. My mother told me 'this is part of history' when it was demolished."

Though the building was gone and the site was cleared out all the way down to the second cellar, the stories of the Underground Railroad stop are still part of St. Johnsbury history.

LUNENBURG

Numerous references state that fugitive slaves crossed the Connecticut River from Littleton, New Hampshire, to Lunenburg, Vermont. It is recorded that Lunenburg was a busy place for receiving fugitives. But where did they go in town, and who helped them?

Four and a half miles south of Lunenburg on Route 2 is the Auburn Star Farm, which was the Spencer Clark farm in the 1800s. The property abuts the Connecticut River banks at an area known as the Clark Bow. The fugitive slave traffic route from Lunenburg continued west to St. Johnsbury and on to Hardwick or Barton.

Spencer Clark, an abolitionist, owned the farm in the 1800s. Clark had a pasture beside the Connecticut River and a tunnel from the fields to the barn, an entrance into a secret cellar and a second-floor hiding place.

The genealogical history compiled on the Clarke-Clark family in 1952, contains a 1924 letter written by Katherine E. Breitling, the great-granddaughter of Ebenezer Clark III, which described Spencer Clark as "an ardent abolitionist."

Clark was the second owner of the stately brick house and farm that his father Ebenezer had built in the 1790s. Clark was known to be a man of strong principles and was involved with his community. He supervised the construction of the Congregational Church in 1850.

Lunenburg's local tradition claims that Clark harbored fugitive slaves that crossed the river from Littleton. In 1992, though the property was an operating farm, the family lived in the brick home, and the original wooden house was not in use and hadn't been renovated in years. Certain physical features were discovered that confirm the stories of secret cellars and concealed hiding places.

Slaves must have come up the river from Littleton by boat at night and unloaded at the bank near the barn. There is a gully in the pasture on the back property that is about twenty feet beyond the barn. Local tradition said this gully was used during pre–Revolutionary War days when settlers hid there from Native American Indians, as a boat landing for general use and also for fugitive slaves.

The barn is forty feet inland from the gully, so fugitive slaves could move up to the barn and then through the barn to the woodshed. The woodshed was connected to the original house but was torn down in the late 1900s.

Then crawling down into an entrance hole beside the house and down into the cellar, they could access the front room near the fireplace through the trapdoor in the floorboards. Clark hid fugitives in the cellar under the original kitchen during the day. If they had to stay longer, they could go to the second floor and hide in the walls. The wall hiding space was only accessible through a small plaster section of the wall that could be pushed out, and they could crawl in between the interior and exterior walls. When it was safe to move to the next point in their journey, Clark would transport them.

Local historian Carol Wenmark stated, "The tunnel by the river was probably there before the 1800s since the house was built in pre–Revolutionary War days. But the tunnel may have been utilized for Underground Railroad use. People have thought they used canoes to transport slaves up the river."

The cellar was not used in recent times since there was only one entrance to it: the trapdoor in the floor. It was thought to be a crawl space only. The outside entrance had caved in years ago. But in 1991, the current owners discovered a three- to four-foot hole next to the house on the side where the trapdoor is located. They found a full cellar, about six feet high.

In the front room, the trapdoor is in the center of the room near the fireplace. There are three two-by-four boards that form a crude trapdoor, covering a hole in the floor. Even today, the two-by-fours stand out because those three boards fit in place with a nail bent over to hold them down.

Of the second-floor hiding space, Breitling referred to the room that the hired farm stayed in as "still another room unfinished, that seemed to me a possible hiding place; just here is an interesting trapdoor. Spencer Clark was an ardent abolitionist and it is just possible some refugee slaves have found here a resting place."

The trapdoor she wrote of is a distinctly marked cutout square on the otherwise smooth plaster wall. It appears to be a section of wall that could be removed, letting fugitives into the secret space.

It wasn't until the chimney in the second-floor room was removed that the hiding place was revealed between the exterior and interior walls. Now you can stand where the chimney once was and look down the length of the building and the hiding space there. The area is approximately six feet high and as wide as the chimney until the roof slants. Then the area is about four feet high and five feet wide, running the length of the original house, twenty to twenty-five feet.

The other interesting feature of this hiding space is that the floor is made of thin boards roughly three inches wide, like slats as in a crate. Open vents along the second floor of a living space don't make sense. Light from outside can be seen through the floor. The floor appeared to be vented, and if slaves were hidden in here with the chimney in place and trapdoor closed, this would be the only way they would have had air circulation and not suffocated.

IN THREE SEPARATE towns on the eastern Vermont border, stories that have been passed down from generation to generation recently aligned and linked the towns to each other. Their common thread was the Underground Railroad efforts to help move fugitive slaves through Orange County, Vermont.

CORINTH

Corinth is a small hamlet in Orange County that is quintessential Vermont with farmlands, hills and forests. It borders Bradford, Topsham, Newbury and Orange. Travelers follow the Waits River east to Barre and continue north to Montpelier and eventually Canada.

In *History of Corinth Vermont 1764–1964*, the Rowland Day place is referred to as an Underground Railroad station for slaves, and the house has a secret room. "Slaves were surreptitiously hurried upstairs to a secret room. To enter, one entered a large bedroom with an open cupboard with many shelves on an inside wall. A strong push on the back wall of the cupboard swung it back like a door, leaving the shelves stationary except for the bottom one which was removable." Through this opening, one could crawl into a small, windowless room that was next to the chimney. On the other side of the chimney was a regular closet.

The current owners, Ed Pospicil and Joie Winchell, said that the previous owners removed the cupboard door of the closet so it is now a second closet space beside the chimney. Neighbors told them stories about playing in the room behind the bookcase cupboard.

Local legend has it that fugitive slaves would arrive at the Rowland Day house and were ushered upstairs to the secret room. Once they crawled inside and the cupboard wall shut, they were hidden until it was time to leave. Then at night, the slaves were sent either by foot or by wagon to their next stop.

The Rowland Day house was built by retired sea captain Richard Rowland, from Lyme, Connecticut, who moved his family of eight children to Corinth. Rowland was a carriage maker in town. The Rowland children married into the Day families of Corinth. It is still known as the Rowland Day house because the Day and Rowland families connected by marriage.

This is the Rowland Day Place in Corinth, owned by Ed Pospicil and Joie Winchell. Father Richard and then son Shalor Rowland lived in the house in the 1800s, and a hidden room next to the chimney existed on the second floor of the house. *Courtesy of Michelle Arnosky Sherburne.*

Descendants of Richard Rowland owned the house for five generations, until the death of Rowland Day in 1963.

As for dates and Underground Railroad connections, Richard Rowland Sr. lived in the house from 1790 to 1823. One of his sons, Shalor, inherited the Rowland Day place and lived there until his death in 1847. Up until Richard Sr. died in 1823, it could have been a family affair with Richard and Shalor aiding fugitives. We do not have the exact documentation to determine that.

When Pospicil and Winchell purchased the house in 1999, the Corinth town historian told them about its Underground Railroad status and also that it was on the route to Topsham, Newbury and then across state lines into Haverhill.

An underground tunnel was built from the basement of a Vermont house out thirty feet, and the tunnel ran under the road to exit in the woods. The construction was elaborate, as evidenced by the granite slabs that weigh approximately one ton and create the roof. The sides of the tunnel are stonewalls. Local tradition is that runaway slaves were taken from the Rowland Day place in Corinth to this house and hidden in the tunnel. Traveling through the tunnel, they could leave unnoticed and were sent to Newbury Village. *Courtesy of Ed Pospicil.*

They were told of a house on the Topsham-Newbury border that had an underground tunnel used for the Underground Railroad. Pospicil was able to visit the house and examine the underground tunnel the Corinth historian spoke of.

An elaborate hidden underground tunnel is connected to the house. The tunnel runs thirty feet out from the house across the yard, and years ago, it ran under the road, coming out in the woods on the other side of the road. This tunnel construction is completely underground, and not many know of its existence. Pospicil said that he was told by a road crew member that when the road was being repaired, part of the tunnel was exposed near the roadway, but then it was filled in.

The tunnel is skillfully constructed, with a ceiling made of granite slabs that rest on full stonewalls. The tunnel is over six feet high and approximately four and a half feet wide. The granite slabs weigh approximately one ton each, so they had to have been brought here by oxen and wagon. The stones for the walls are not rough fieldstones but rounded, water-worn stones, meaning they must have been brought to the location.

The entrance to the tunnel is behind cellar shelving in the house cellar. The tunnel extends thirty feet out from the basement. But it is unnoticeable when walking on the lawn behind the house.

Why would this construction be done in the first place? Is it a root cellar for storing vegetables year-round? Too elaborate and large for that purpose. Is it a storage area off from the basement? There is no record that it was the foundation of a section of the house or woodshed or outbuilding. Was it used for runaway slaves or smuggling of some kind?

This tunnel clearly exists and was constructed for a reason and for a specific purpose. It could have been built for another reason but used for slaves simply because it was there, like the Spring Hotel tunnel in the next section.

Local tradition has it that runaways were instructed to go through the Topsham-Newbury tunnel and head to the railroad tracks and follow them

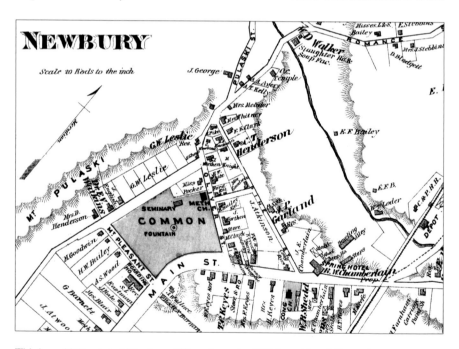

This is an 1877 print of Newbury Village from the *F.W. Beers Atlas of Orange County, Vermont.* The map shows the Spring Hotel, the bank where the tunnel entrance is (not drawn on the map) and the railroad tracks in the gully north of the hotel. It also has the Newbury Common with the Newbury Seminary and Methodist Episcopal Church featured there. *Courtesy of Dave Allen at www.old-maps.com, P.O. Box 54, West Chesterfield, New Hampshire, 03466.*

into a village—Newbury, to be exact. Up on the bank from the railroad tracks they would see a four-story hotel. On the hotel bank was a tunnel entrance, which they could crawl through under the main road in the village and come out the other side into a hole in a house lawn. There they would be helped across the river to the Bliss Tavern, a safe house in Haverhill.

NEWBURY

The landmark given to slaves heading for Newbury was the former Spring Hotel on North Main Street, across from the First Congregational Church in Newbury Village. The Spring Hotel burned in 1879, and the Tenney Memorial Library was built and today is on that site on Route 5 in the village.

The Spring Hotel was built in 1800 and became a popular summer resort with healing springs in the gulley beside the property. The hotel underwent numerous renovations throughout its history. One in particular occurred in 1810, when proprietor Edward Little added a third story, and in the *History of Newbury, Vt.*, it recorded that there were "secret rooms reached by a winding passage around one of the chimneys. The rooms were furnished with huge chests for smuggled goods during the era of the War of 1812 when smuggling was profitable and a thriving side business."

The tunnel entrance still exists on the steep wooded bank, well concealed by a stone wall and trees. The bank leads to a gulley where the railroad track runs through town.

It is a carefully constructed brick archway constructed of two layers of bricks, with a seven-foot-tall arch that is eight feet wide and ten feet deep. It has three brick walls, a ceiling and a dirt floor, and the actual tunnel had a small door. (Twenty years ago it was still there but not in place, but now it is gone.) The tunnel opening was filled in with dirt years ago to prevent kids from playing in the tunnel.

The tunnel was large enough for an adult male to crouch and travel through. The late Dorothea Mayo owned the property where the tunnel opening was located. She said that the opening on the other side of the road was a hole inlaid with bricks as big around as a barrel cover and covered with a slab. The tunnel hole was only a few feet from the bank that drops down to the fields next to the Connecticut River; across the way is Haverhill.

The hole on Mayo's property was paved over in 1991. In 1992, Mayo shared that local tradition said that the tunnel was used by runaway slaves

A tunnel ran under the former Spring Hotel in the 1800s in Newbury, and its entrance still exists on the side of the bank. The carefully crafted structure is made of bricks and is ten feet into the bank and seven feet tall. The tunnel opening and its exit on the other side of Route 5 were filled in years ago. *Courtesy of* Caledonian-Record, *August 1992, photo by Michelle Arnosky Sherburne.*

to get through the village either coming from or going to the Bliss Tavern in Haverhill.

The tunnel itself was probably built in 1869 when hotel owner Samuel Kendall introduced illuminating gas at the hotel. The Vermont Historical Society told Mayo that the tunnel was used for that purpose only. Mayo had said that the hotel was known for smuggling during the War of 1812, and it was said the tunnel was used for smuggling slaves.

Mayo's house was originally the Shedd House, built in the late 1780s by Timothy Shedd. His son, William Shedd, lived in Newbury all his life. William was a banker, town representative, state senator and director of the state prison. He died in 1885. When fugitives were directed to Newbury Village, they could have been aided by William.

Newbury residents share stories about fugitive slaves coming through town and other locations come up in conversation—Colonel Thomas Johnson's house on the Oxbow, the Swasey House two houses south of Oxbow Cemetery and the underground room at the slaughterhouse.

Romance Lane's Underground Room

Not far from the tunnel location is Romance Lane and the Dorothy Edson property. The Edson property was the site of the 1800s slaughterhouse and soap factory owned by W.D. Walker. An underground room was discovered in the 1980s when the late Mac Knight, longtime Newbury resident, was excavating the property to install a new septic system. The site he was digging was where a barn used to be beside the house.

Beyond the basement wall of the Edson house, old timbers for an underground room with stonewalls and a wooden ceiling were uncovered by Knight's crew. The room was large enough to hold approximately thirty people, and there were benches, still intact, around the outside walls. Three walls of the underground room were made of stone, and the fourth wall was the slaughterhouse basement wall. Access to this hidden room, Knight surmised, was the easily removable stones on the back wall.

Knight had heard stories of a secret room on the property being used to hide slaves. Fugitives would travel from Haverhill, somewhere along the riverbank, hide there, and move into Newbury where they were hidden under the slaughterhouse for safety.

Unfortunately, the secret room was reburied since the septic system was more important at the time.

HAVERHILL, NEW HAMPSHIRE

Bliss Tavern

Crossing from Newbury into New Hampshire, fugitive slaves were sent to the Bliss Tavern. Haverhill is one of those towns that surfaces in many Underground Railroad texts: "Taken to Haverhill and passed north to Littleton" or "the runaway slaves went from Canaan, Lyme and up to Haverhill."

This is where local historians and descendants fill in the information and the story is uncovered. The safe house was Bliss Tavern on the Haverhill Common, and Timothy Blaisdell was the Underground Railroad agent. He received fugitive slaves from Newbury or from Lyme, New Hampshire agents who traveled seventeen miles to deliver them to Blaisdell.

The Bliss Tavern on the Haverhill Commons in Haverhill, New Hampshire, is a well-known Underground Railroad station. Its owner in the 1800s was Timothy Blaisdell, who received fugitive slaves from Lyme agents. He sent them across the Connecticut River to Newbury, Vermont, or took them north toward Littleton, New Hampshire. *Courtesy of Michelle Arnosky Sherburne.*

The Bliss Tavern was a busy stop on a stagecoach route in the 1800s. The building's history includes use as a tavern, post office commissioned by President George Washington and original courthouse in Grafton County. Even the famous Massachusetts statesman and senator Daniel Webster frequented the Bliss so regularly that the Blaisdells had a room designated for him. Today it is still called the Daniel Webster Room.

In the *History of the Town of Haverhill*, Blaisdell is referred to as "a pronounced Abolitionist." He was a member of the American Anti-slavery Society. Mildred C. Paulsen, Blaisdell's granddaughter, wrote a letter to Wilbur Siebert in 1935 about Underground Railroad activity. She reported that her grandfather was a "very earnest worker for the cause and he made the remark once that the proudest moment of his life was when he was 'rotten egged' on Boston Common for making a speech on abolition." He was involved in the New Hampshire Antislavery and the American Antislavery Societies.

One of Blaisdell's daughters, Harriet Blaisdell Cram, passed along accounts of seeing fugitive slaves when she was growing up. These were recorded in the *History of Haverhill*, written in the late 1890s.

144

Paulsen wrote, "Many of the slaves came to grandfather from Boston… [he was] the only person in town who received and cared for the fugitives and sent them on to Littleton or some other town north of here."

Betty Johnson Gray and Arthur Gray bought the Bliss Tavern in the late 1970s. She had heard of its Underground Railroad connection while living in Lyme and was told by Charles Balch that his grandfather had "taken twelve slaves in a wagon pulled by a team of oxen, to Bliss Tavern where they were hidden around the chimney in the attic." Gray said, "I was fascinated with the history of this house. I went to Dartmouth libraries to learn all I could about the Underground Railroad. I fell in love with the house when I visited and was given a tour."

The physical features of the Bliss Tavern still exist: a tunnel entrance, cellar storage unit, a first-floor closet with stairs six feet off the ground leading to the ceiling and into a second-floor pantry that take one to a trapdoor and a large hiding area around the center chimney in the attic.

The cellar has an opening in the wall that is the beginning of a tunnel that ran under the Haverhill Common to the bank on the other side of Route 10 where the meadows lead down to the Connecticut River.

The first floor closet is directly under a pantry closet on the second floor built beside the center chimney. The first-floor closet stairs, that start six feet from the floor, lead to the ceiling, where two of the ceiling boards are removable, creating an entrance into a second-floor pantry. In the second-floor pantry, there is a Dutch oven and dumbwaiter for a ballroom on the second floor. The pantry is built around the center chimney. On the right side of the chimney, the bricks are terraced and the space is six feet high. Up that terraced space, there is a trapdoor that leads to the attic. Gray said, "Once in the attic space, the slaves were hidden in the large area around the chimney, as many as twelve at a time."

READING

In 1995, father and son, Steve and Steven Leninski were digging near their 1800s farmhouse, and they unearthed two incredible archaeological finds: a two-pound, hand-forged circle of iron, hinged at one side with a small hasp on the other side and a pair of Colonial-era iron scissors.

They had been digging under what had been granite steps descending into the original 1807 farmhouse basement when they unearthed the collar

While digging near the Woodstock farmhouse foundation, Steve Leninski and his father dug up two fascinating artifacts: a two-pound, hand-forged slave collar, hinged at one side with a small hasp, and also a pair of Colonial-era iron scissors. It was August 1995, and ten feet down, they uncovered history. The slave collar had been cut, and the iron scissor tips were broken. They surmised that a fugitive slave had stopped at the farm and used the scissors to free himself. *Courtesy of Eric Francis,* Rutland Herald, *May 6, 2001, "Weight of History" and collar in Steve Leninski private collection.*

and scissors. "It is amazing that these historic items came out of the ground. The scissors' tips were broken off. The metal used was heavy and it was obvious that the collar had been forged and crafted well," said son Steve.

The iron collar is similar to what some slaves wore. There is a series of hash marks around the outside of the collar halves. The steady pattern suggests an identification or branding code that may have identified a specific slave owner, or it could be the markings of the blacksmith who forged it. They had it evaluated by Alvin Montgomery at Columbia University, and it was found to be authentic. "The collar was encrusted in clay, which preserved it so well," said son Steve.

How did the slave collar and scissors end up in the earth in Vermont? Slave collars were worn by new slaves coming into America or used as a way to cuff slave workers together working on a chain gang, and slaves on sale may have worn collars to transport them to the auction block. With the iron scissors found near the collar, it is surmised that the slave collar was cut off at the spot of the farmhouse.

Steve researched to find out more about the past to possibly explain this incredible find. The farmhouse was built by Henry Walker in 1807. Walker had a black farmhand working for him named Silas Burdoo from approximately 1832 until 1900.

Burdoo's father was Aaron Burdoo, who was born in Lexington, Massachusetts, and may have been a slave prior to the Revolutionary War but was freed thereafter. Aaron Burdoo moved to Reading, Vermont, in 1784 with his wife and bought approximately twenty-six lots of land, some of which were seventy-acre lots.

In the *1790 Heads of Families at the First Census of the United States,* listed under Windsor County, Town of Reading, are two Burdoo households. Aaron Burdoo is recorded has having three "other free persons" in his household, and a Silas Burdoo, Aaron's brother, is also listed with a household of three.

Aaron's son Silas, named after his uncle, was born in Reading in 1826. Aaron died in 1832, and nothing is mentioned about the Burdoo family continuing to own the vast acreage he had obtained. What is known is that Silas was six years old when his father died, and he immediately went to work for a neighbor farmer, Henry Walker. This working relationship continued throughout Silas's entire life.

What became of the rest of the family is unknown. But the son, Silas, never owned property and never received an "inheritance" of the land his father once owned. Whether the ownership was absorbed by Walker or someone else in the town of Reading is unknown but assumed.

During the Civil War, Walker then paid Silas $300 to fight in his place. Silas is listed with the Vermont recruits for the famous Fifty-fourth Massachusetts Colored Unit, established by Robert Shaw. Burdoo is listed as from Woodstock and was thirty-seven when he enlisted on December 19, 1863.

He was wounded and hospitalized in South Carolina. Silas suffered from rheumatism, heart problems and arthritis. He was discharged in 1865 and returned to the Walker farm. Leninski has the records and medical papers of Silas's attempts to get a war pension. Testimonial letters from neighbors were delivered to White River military officials for review, but Silas never received what he deserved. Silas died in 1900 at age seventy-four and was buried on the premises.

As for the slave collar and iron scissors found, they had been on someone, cut off, buried and hidden for decades. Their story remains a mystery.

AFTERWORD

Through years of research, it has been amazing to learn about the Underground Railroad. Stories, documents and artifacts continue to surface enabling us to learn more of the layers of our country's history.

The fugitive slaves were the real heroes, determined to be free. Many died trying to escape. Many suffered recapture and return to slavery. They fought for what they knew was their right to be free. Their triumph was the Thirteenth Amendment, which abolished slavery in our country.

As we have learned, Vermont had its own layers of abolition and Underground Railroad activity. Just like the other Underground Railroad networks in the Northern states, Vermonters put themselves on the line for strangers, knowing the risk and the consequences. They helped the slaves any way they could and became a part of the Underground Railroad network.

The Underground Railroad is an important part of our country's history, and I hope this book has shed some light on Vermonters' roles.

BIBLIOGRAPHY

Allen, Mrs. M.F. "In Memoriam, Rowland E. Robinson." *The Vermonter*, December 1900.

Armstrong, Margaret B., Pamela J. Caldwell and Dorothy C. Steele. *St. Albans, Vermont, Through the Years, 1763–1963; A Bicentennial History*. St. Albans, VT: St. Albans Historical Society, 1977.

Baldwin, Jessie A. *History & Folklore of Post Mills, VT.* Thetford, VT: Thetford Historical Society, 1983.

Berlin, Ira. *Slaves Without Masters, The Free Negro in the Antebellum South*. New York: New Press, 1974.

Bittinger, Reverend J.Q. *History of Haverhill, NH*. Haverhill, NH: Cohos Steam Press, 1888.

Blackburn, Maria. "The Legends of the Underground Railroad." *Burlington Free Press*, March 24, 1996.

Blaisdell, Katharine. *Over the River and Through the Years Book 1–6, from the Journal Opinion, Bradford, VT, and Woodsville, NH*. N.p., 1983.

Blight, David W. *Passage to Freedom; Underground Railroad in History and Memory*. New York: HarperCollins, 2006.

Blockson, Charles L. *The Underground Railroad*. Upper Saddle River, NJ: Prentice Hall, 1987.

Bogart, Ernest L. *Peacham: The Story of a Vermont Hill Town*. Montpelier: Vermont Historical Society, 1948.

Brainerd, Lucy Abigail. *The Geneaology of the Brainerd, Brainerd Family of America 1649–1908*, 3 vol. Hartford, CT: Case, Lockwood and Brainard, 1908.

Buckmaster, Henrietta. *Let My People Go.* New York: Harper and Brothers, 1966 (1941 original).

Byington, Ezra Hoyt, and Gilbert Asa Davis. *History of the First Congregational Church of Windsor, Vermont, 1768–1898.* Windsor, VT: Journal Company, 1898.

Calarco, Tom. "The Underground Railroad in Vermont after 1850." www.suite101.com, April 3, 2010.

Canfield, Mary Grace. *The Valley of Kedron, the Story of the South Parish, Woodstock, VT.* South Woodstock, VT: Kedron Associates, 1940.

"The Cause in Vermont." *The Liberator,* September 21, 1860.

Cheney, Cora. *Vermont, The State with the Storybook Past.* Brattleboro, VT: S. Greene Press, 1976.

Child, Hamilton. *Gazeteer of Caledonia and Essex Counties, VT, 1764–1887.* Syracuse, NY: Syracuse Journal Co., Printers and Binders, 1887.

Chryssi, George. "American Philhellenes and the War for Independence." *Hellenic Voice,* March 20, 2002.

Dana, Henry Swan. *History of Woodstock, VT.* New York: Houghton Mifflin, 1889.

Davis, Gilbert A. *History of Reading, Windsor County, Vermont, Vol. II.* [Windsor, VT]: N.p., 1903.

Divine, Robert A. *America Past and Present, Volume I to 1877.* New York: Pearson Longman, 2005.

Dorman, Franklin A. *Twenty Families of Color in Massachusetts 1742–1988.* Boston: New England Historic Geneology Society, 1998.

Douglass, Frederick. *Life and Times of Frederick Douglass: From 1817–1882, written by Himself, John Libb, John Bright.* London, Christian Age Office, 1882.

Eisan, Frances K. *Saint or Demon? The Legendary Delia Webster Opposing Slavery.* New York: Pace University Press, 1998.

"Escape from Slavery." *National Geographic* 166, no. 1 (July 1984).

Fisher, Sally. "In Pursuit of Reverend Bayley." *Hazen Road Dispatch* 10 (Summer 1985).

"Former Vermont Governor's Burial Site," *VOCA (Vermont Old Cemetery Association) News,* Fall 1994.

Francis, Eric. "Weight of History." *Rutland Herald, Sunday Magazine,* May 6, 2001.

Gara, Larry. *The Liberty Line: The Legend of the Underground Railroad.* Lexington: University of Kentucky Press, 1967.

Gerzina, Gretchen Holbrook. *Mr. and Mrs. Prince: How an Extraordinary Eighteenth-Century Family Moved Out of Slavery and Into Legend.* New York: Amistad, 2008.

Goodwillie, John Ross. *The Goodwillies 1590–1986: Four Hundred Years of Family History.* Islington, Ontario: self-published, 1986.

Greeley, Horace. *Recollections of a Busy Life*. New York: J.B. Ford and Co., 1868.

Guyette, Elise A. *Discovering Black Vermont: African American Farmers in Hinesburgh, 1790–1890*. Burlington: University of Vermont Press, University Press of New England, 2010.

Hahn, Michael. *Alexander Twilight: Vermont's African American Pioneer*. Shelburne, VT: New England Press, 1998.

Heaton, E.N. *A Brief History of the Post Mills Congregational Church*. Bradford, VT: Press of the Opinion, 1920.

Hemenway, Abby Maria, and Brenda Morrissey. *Unique Portrait of a State: Abby Hemenway's Vermont*. Brattleboro, VT: S. Greene Press, 1972.

Hemenway, Abigail Maria. *Vermont Historical Gazetteer in 3 Volumes*. N.p., 1867.

Historic Houses of Springfield, Vermont. Springfield, VT: Historical Committee of the Miller Art Center, n.d.

Hubbard, C. Horace, and Justus Dartt. *History of the Town of Springfield*. Boston: Geo. H. Walker, 1895.

Jackson, James Robert, and George Clarence Furber. *History of Littleton, NH in 3 Volumes*. Vol. 1. N.p., 1905.

Johnson, Claire Dunne. *I See by the Papers*. St. Johnsbury, VT: self-published, 1987.

Ledoux, Rodney L. *History of Swanton, Vermont*. Swanton, VT: Swanton Historical Society, 1988.

"Letters of William Lloyd Garrison: From Disunionism to the Brink of War, 1850–1860 Letters." Cambridge: Belknap Press of Harvard University Press, 1971–1981. Accessed on Google documents.

Louisville Democrat. "Difficulties with Delia Webster," July 18, 1854. Copyright *New York Times*.

Lovejoy, John M. "Racism in Antebellum Vermont." *Vermont History*, 2001.

Muller, H.N., and Samuel B. Hand. *In a State of Nature: Reading in Vermont History*. Montpelier: Vermont Historical Society, 1982.

Northrup, Solomon. *Twelve Years A Slave: Narrative of Solomon Northrup*. 1853. Chapel Hill: University of North Carolina, 2011.

Orange County Court Records, vol. 13, pp. 208–10.

"Prayer of Rev. Young." *New York Daily Tribune*, December 12, 1859.

Raffo, Steven. *A Biography of Oliver Johnson, Abolitionist and Reformer 1809–1889*. Lewiston, NY: Edwin Mellen Press, 2002.

"Re-enactment of John Brown's Funeral." www.johnbrownsbody.net. July 10, 1997.

Robinson, Rowland E. *Out of Bondage and Other Stories, Centennial Edition*. Edited by Llewellyn R. Perkins. Rutland, VT: Charles E. Tuttle Co., 1936.

"Rodney Marsh Famous Home Is at Brandon." *Rutland Herald*, May 31, 1939.

Ross, Dr. Alexander Milton. *Recollections and Experiences of An Abolitionist from 1855 to 1865*. Toronto: Rowsell and Hutchinson, 1816.

Roth, Randolph. "Can Faith Change the World? Religion and Society in Vermont's Age of Reform." *Vermont History*, 2001.

Runyon, Randolph Paul. *Delia Webster and the Underground Railroad*. Lexington: University Press of Kentucky, 1996.

"Safford's Straw Cutter." *The Farmer*, March 29, 1823.

Saunders, Richard H., and Virginia M. Westbrook. *Celebrating Vermont: Myths and Realities*. Middlebury, VT: University Press of New England, 1991.

Siebert, Wilbur. *Underground Railroad: From Slavery to Freedom*. Original 1898. New York: Peter Smith, reprint 1968.

———. *Vermont's Anti-Slavery and Underground Railroad Record with a Map and Illustrations*. Columbus, OH: Spahr and Glenn, 1937.

Smedley, R.C. *History of the Underground Railroad in Chester and The Neighboring Counties of Pennsylvania*. New York: Negro Universities Press, 1883.

Stein, Conrad R. *Story of the Underground Railroad*. Chicago: Children's Press, 1981.

Still, William. *The Underground Railroad*. Philadelphia: People's Publishing Company, 1878.

Stone, Arthur F. *The Vermont of Today, Vol. I*. New York: Lewis Historical Publishing Company, 1929.

Thompson, D.P. *History of the Town of Montpelier*. Montpelier, VT: E.P. Walton, 1860.

Town of Corinth Historical Society. *History of Corinth, Vermont 1764–1964*. Corinth, VT: self-published, 1995.

Wells, Frederick. *History of Newbury 1704–1902*. N.p., n.d.

Wells, Frederick P. *History of Barnet, Vermont*. Burlington, VT: Free Press, 1923.

Whitcher, William F. *History of the Town of Haverhill, NH*. Concord, NH: Rumford Press, 1919.

Wickham, Elizabeth Merwin. *A Lost Family Found: An Authentic Narrative of Cyrus Branch and His Family, Alias John White of Manchester, Vermont*. Chapel Hill: University of North Carolina, electronic edition, www.docsouth.nc.edu.

Wikoff, Jerold. *The Upper Valley, An Illustrated Tour Along the Connecticut River Before the Twentieth Century*. Chelsea, VT: Chelsea Green, 1985.

Williamson, Jane. "A Private Museum Confronts the Underground Railroad." *Vermont History*.

———. "Rowland T. Robinson, Rokeby and the Underground Railroad in Vermont," *Vermont History* 69 (Winter 2001).

————. "Telling It Like It Was: The Evolution of an Underground Railroad Historic Site," *Vermont History.*

Winter, Kari J. *The Blind African Slave.* Madison: University of Wisconsin Press, 2004.

Youngwood, Susan. "Unearthing the Underground Railroad: Where Does Myth End and Reality Begin?" *Vermont Life*, Summer 1999.

Zirblis, Raymond Paul. "Friends of Freedom: The Vermont Underground Survey Report." State of Vermont, Vermont Department of State Buildings and Vermont Division for Historic Preservation, 1996.

NEWSPAPERS

Herald of Freedom, July 9, 1836.
Herald of Freedom, November 28, 1836.
Liberator, October 31, 1835.
Newport (NH) Spectator, September 1835.
NH Patriot and State Gazette, October 12, 1835.
State Journal, October 27, 1835.

COLLECTIONS

Barnet Historical Society collection.
Peacham Historical Society collection.
Rokeby Museum letter collection, Robinson family letters.
Wilbur H. Siebert Underground Railroad Collection by Ohio Historical Society available on www.ohiomemory.org.

WEBSITES

www.ancestryarchives.com.
"Bigelow Family Genealogy." www.BigelowSociety.com.
"Documenting the American South." www.docsouth.unc.edu
www.footnote.com.
http://northcountryundergroundrailroad.com.

www.theliberatorfiles.com
www.vermontcivilwar.org.
www.vermonthistory.org.
www.virtualvermont.com.

INDEX

W

ABOUT THE AUTHOR

Michelle Arnosky Sherburne lives with her husband and son in Newbury, Vermont. She is a Vermont historian and has spent years researching the Underground Railroad and the Civil War, lecturing at schools and local organizations. Michelle co-authored *A Vermont Hill Town in the Civil War: Peacham's Story* and is a freelance writer for newspapers and magazines. She works at a weekly newspaper when not on history quests.